Sex, Dating and Love

The questions most often asked

Ray E. Short

Author of the Bestseller
SEX, LOVE, OR INFATUATION

Augsburg
MINNEAPOLIS

SEX, DATING, AND LOVE
The Questions Most Often Asked

Cover design: Lecy Design
Interior design: James F. Brisson

Library of Congress Cataloging-in-Publication Data

Short, Ray E.
    Sex, dating, and love : the questions most often asked / Ray
E. Short.
      p.   cm.
    "Second edition."
    ISBN 0-8066-2708-5 :
    1. Dating (Social customs).   2. Love.   3. Sex.   I. Title.
HQ801.S53   1994
306.7—dc20   94-10412
                                                           CIP

The paper used in this publication meets the minimum require-
ments of American National Standard for Information Sciences—
Permanence of Paper for Printed Library Materials, ANSI
Z329.48-1984.   ∞ ™

Manufactured in the U.S.A.   AF 9-2708

98   97   96   95   94   1   2   3   4   5   6   7   8   9   10

DEDICATIONS

To my wife of 40 years,
JEANNETTE;

to the 300,000+ young people
who have shared their questions and deep concerns,
without which this book would not exist, and to

HERB LUSCOMBE and
HENRY BURTON SHARMAN,
who led me into religion,

HORNELL HART,
who led me into science, and

HERMAN CLARK,
who helped me put them together.

CONTENTS

PART 3: **How Old Is Old Enough? – 46**

PART 4: **Dating Not for Mating – 52**

7

8

PART 8: **Teen Sex: Time to Sound the Alarm**

PART 10: **The Problem of Pregnancy** – 137

PART 12: **Can Boozer Choosers Be Losers?** – 154

PART 13: **STDs: Those Antisocial Social Diseases** – 158

PART 14: **AIDS: The Killer STD** – 167

PART 16: **The Guilt Trip Trauma** — 203

The need for this book seems crystal clear. That has been proved to me over and over in past years from my own and other research. The youth and college students want straight answers, and they deserve to get just that.

This book really belongs to young people. They have shaped its content. Here's how it happened.

In the past few years I have addressed many hundreds of groups. More than a third of a million youth and students have been in attendance. They included, for the most part, high school—and even junior high—assemblies, youth conferences, and college, university, and vo-tech programs. Some were groups of parents, workers with youth, or professionals. But mostly I speak to youth themselves. And it is from them that the data and the inspiration for this book have come. The pattern is as follows.

After each presentation the audience is given blank cards. These all look the same. All persons are invited to "write any questions you wish about dating, courtship, *sex*, going steady, *sex*" (and they get the point!). They are not to reveal in any way who's asking what question. No matter what they ask, if it's a serious question I promise to give them a straight answer and do it without mumbling.

When they get the chance to ask any question at all and still remain anonymous, they really ask what is on their minds. Questions are then drawn at random from the pack. This book is for the most part made up of answers to those questions asked most often by youth today. I trust that it will be of help not only to young people, but to all who work closely with them. Parents and others can find here the questions their young are asking.

18

Counselors, pastors, friends of youth, and teachers in schools and churches should find the book useful. If both youth and their elders read it, that could open the lines of communication and lead to solid sex education in home, church, and school. That is, it could help parents and youth to talk frankly in the home about sex, love, and responsibility. Schools and youth groups can find materials here for endless discussions in classes or meetings. Young people can talk over the book's contents in their private conversations and work out their own answers.

I have brought to this book the viewpoints of both science and religion. I do not see these as being in conflict; rather they complement each other. Religious zeal needs to be tempered by the hard facts of scientific research, lest it lose touch with the realities of our times. But the cold facts of science need to be softened by the warmth of religion's concern for moral values and meaning in life, and its constant caring for human beings and their needs. Science brings knowledge; religion brings wisdom—the right use of that knowledge.

The need is to join these two together. I have tried to do just that. I write as a practicing social scientist with over 30 years' experience teaching college courses on marriage and the family here and abroad. I have made an effort always to present solid facts based on valid research.

I have also purposely sought to steer clear of preachiness and moralizing. That approach, I find, tends to turn off this generation of youth and young adults. Instead, I try to provide the facts needed by the reader to make his or her own decisions.

At the same time, I write as one who since early adulthood has been dedicated to the service of the will of our Judeo-Christian God. We hold that God is good, and that life is good—a sacred gift. That means that our whole selves—our minds, our spirits, our emotions, our social lives, our bodies (and yes, our sexuality)—are all good when

19

rightly used. God wants for each of us the best that life can bring.

This is a great generation of young people. They are open and they are smart. But at the same time they are troubled. They want to do the right thing with their lives, and they are looking for straight answers based on sound scientific facts. And if they are given honest answers, most of them will try to shape their lives accordingly. If these pages serve to help them reach that goal, this author will be pleased.

Why does this book need a second edition?

Changes in Our Thinking—and Our Actions

Rapid changes have occurred in the thinking and the behavior of our youth and, indeed, their elders. Now, people are much more tolerant of living-in prior to marriage. A decade or so ago about 500,000 persons lived together. Now over two million do so.[1]

More teenagers—and even adults—think sex before marriage is OK. And they now do it more often, and at younger and younger ages.

Year by year, unwed under-age pregnancies reach new highs. Sexually transmitted diseases (STDs) have reached epidemic levels among the young, and keep getting worse. And, of course, if they get AIDS, it will—at least as of now—kill them.

People seem to be influenced much more by the moral values—or lack of them—put forth by the media, than by all the values found in their family, church, and school put together. All of these critical issues will be dealt with more fully in this edition.

Most of the youth who do get into sex take few if any precautions to help avoid the risks. Those who do, place far more faith in condoms and "the pill" than is wise. If they know that there is no such thing as "safe sex" (except abstinence), they do not take it to heart. And while the spread of AIDS in 1992 by homosexuals and needle-users remained quite stable, AIDS spread by male-female sex rose an alarming 17 percent. Thus many experts predict that in the 1990s, AIDS will spread more rapidly among our teenagers than among any other group.

Like it or not, these trends are very real. If we are to increase our efforts to help youth and others make sound choices, we need to face these facts. The problems won't just go away. Young people need to know how to avoid choices that will risk messing up their lives. Such risks may even lead to their early death. I hope the update of this book will help guide young people in making sound choices. And it can help those who love and care about them to better serve their needs as well.

Does This Shock You?

Let's face it. The questions the young people now ask clearly reflect their increased involvement in sex. That should come as no surprise. Of the 40,000–60,000 anonymous questions I now get each year when I speak, more and more are about actually having sex: What's the best kind of birth control? What's the best condom to use? Where can I get them? Is withdrawal a safe method? When is a woman least likely to get pregnant? Why is premarital sex wrong? Isn't sex OK if the couple love each other? What position is the best one for sex? Isn't it better to try out sex before you marry? Or live together first?

We have to assume such queries are not just out of idle curiosity. It shows they are already doing it—or at least wanting to or planning to.

Sometimes when I speak at a high school, I gather a group of the students and ask: "What is your best guess as to the percentage of your students that are sexually active right now?" No student group guesses that it is less than 50 percent. I get the same results even in parochial high schools where moral training is part of the curriculum. Counselors tell me that these student estimates are, in fact, in the ball park.

Some students are not into full intercourse, but they are involved with other kinds of sexual activity. They ask questions that are even more blunt: Will it hurt the first time I have sex? Will it hurt less if I'm drunk? Is it OK to have oral (mouth-to-genital) sex? What does the 6-9 position mean (couples giving each other oral sex at the same time)? Is it OK to have anal sex?

Such questions reflect one stark fact. More and more youth—even those with religious backgrounds—do experiment with such behaviors. And at younger and younger ages.

A decade ago, one would expect to get such questions only from those who were married, engaged, or living together WBC (without benefit of clergy). Not any more.

Readers may be shocked that such questions are so common from such young students. I'm not. After fielding hundreds of thousands of questions over the past 19 years, they just can't shock me anymore—though some of them keep giving it their best shot.

"Why Do You Talk to Kids About Sex?"

Why do I bother? The answer is quite simple. I want to give people the kind of facts, based on solid research, that could help them make smart choices. Far too many fine young people are risking their very lives and future for the immediate thrills of sex. If through my books, programs, and media interviews I can help pave the way for happy marriages and fruitful lives, that will be my reward. No one gave me straight answers when I was young. How I wish they had! But since even today, far too few young people and their elders get that kind of help, I want to do my very best to fill that void. And all the evidence seems to show that we may be getting through to the youth in my speaking and the books.

Up to 66 percent of a high school student body will move toward abstinence from sex as the result of my program. To me that is astounding. At the same time, it is most gratifying. Since we need many more people out there getting these results, I now hold training seminars in Colorado every July. I hope to teach others how to get these results.

My former dean at the University of Wisconsin, Dr. Bruce Crowell, once told me: "Ray, signs of a considerably more mature, less frivolous approach to this crucial subject (of sex and love) are emerging. I believe that you have contributed powerfully to this turnaround, through your books, . . . your outstanding workshops among countless high schools all over the country, and through your skillfully developed seminars for counselors and youth workers. We wish there were 1,000 like you out there working, but we are profoundly grateful there is at least one." We just hope he's right. We will train as many as we can.

The need is indeed great. But it is tough trying to compete with the cheap, sleazy, purely physical media concepts of sex that constantly bombard our youth. And these messages give not one hint of the tragedies that may follow. We need all the help we can get to counter this negative influence on our young.

In this revised edition we have added a whole new section on AIDS. We use the term STD instead of the older concept, venereal disease (VD), which has gone out of style. Of course, no matter how we may try to clean up the title, the tragic effects of these diseases remain just as bad.

The material progresses from the more basic questions asked by the youngest readers to the more complex ones asked by those who are more mature, including marrieds. I see the book as a valuable tool to help parents teach their children sound facts about sex and love that young people want—and need—to know.

Warm thanks are due those who have checked the early copies of the manuscript for factual accuracy and literary content: Dr. Orval Nelson, marriage counselor, and high school teacher Virginia Clark Teemer.

Deep gratitude is also due the countless persons who have asked those marvelous anonymous questions. Without them neither edition of this book could have been possible. Special thanks must go to my dear wife of 40 years, Jeannette, for all her advice and help. And she holds down the home front while her life mate is out pointing the young towards abstinence, good marriages, high self-esteem, and sound sexual choices. If you should, by chance, want me to speak, do call me at 303-666-5025.

R.E.S.

PART 1

Is the Urge a Scourge?

1 Why is there such a thing as sex?

Some may think your question is too simple. I don't. I think you hear so much degrading talk of sex, see so many problems, so much senseless hype about sex, that it gets tiresome. You just wish the whole thing would go away. We've gone sex crazy in our country.

But sex used in the right way is both necessary and good. Sex has two fine purposes.

First, if there were no such thing as sex, this would be the last group of humans on this earth. As of now, I see little chance of that happening. Our problem is not the threat of too few folks in this world, but too many.

And think about this. Sex actually allows each one of us to be a co-creator with the Great Creator of another wonderful little person. What a privilege! What a joy! What a miracle! What a wondrous gift—the gift of another human life is in our hands! And that life comes from a female ovum so small it can pass through a tube with an opening only slightly larger than a human hair. The sperm that joins the ovum is even smaller. It is one of about 100-500 million contained in about one liquid drop of the male semen. How foolish of us to misuse and abuse this precious gift! As Hornell Hart used to tell his students: "How dare you look upon sex as just a plaything!"

Yet sex is being misused. It has been seen as just a plaything. And what a price we do pay! Misuse of sex has led to a whole host of tragic results. Unwanted pregnancy. Forced marriages that don't work. Abortions by the millions. Poor marriages. Divorce. Sexually transmitted diseases (STDs), some of which have no cure and can even kill. The list goes on.

But sex has a second good purpose. It is a precious gift to two people who really love each other and are committed long term to each other. Sex is a beautiful way for people to express their love and caring for their mate. And if a child comes, it will have two devoted, loving parents to give it a stable home.

True, if used in wrong and selfish ways, sex can be our downfall. It can lead to misery and poverty of our spirits and severe problems for our society. But in the right context, in the safety and security of marriage, sex can be a long-term joy and a source of great satisfaction. I call this the "sanctity of sex."

Now can you see why we were given this wonderful gift of sex?

2 Are you weird if you daydream about sex in the middle of the day? Or as one girl put it: Why do guys always think about sex?

They do. One study found that at ages 12–19, young males think about sex about once every five minutes.[1] If that makes a person weird, then there certainly are a lot of weirdos in this world.

Men are much more likely to think often about sex than women. Most women would be terribly shocked if they knew just how often in a day the average man thinks about sex. And some men, sadly enough, mentally undress almost all the women they meet.

No, to think about sex is not at all rare. Of course this is more likely to happen at times when a person's sex passion has been aroused. And infatuated persons tend to do more than their share of "wool gathering."

Daydreams about sex are quite normal, but there is need for one note of caution here. If you "have sex" with another person in your daydreams, it may lead you to want to follow through and make those dreams come true. If you or the other person are married, you are "committing adultery with her [or him] in your heart," as Jesus put it. And that is just plain wrong.

Why is that so? Because when you see the other person as just a sex object, you make that person less than human. He or she is seen not as a living, breathing, thinking human being. They become a thing, as just a possible outlet for your own sex urges. It cheapens both you as a person, and your view of that other person.

While sex fantasies are normal, if you do too much of it you may wish to reconsider. You might ask yourself whether there are better uses to which you can put your time and that wondrous mind of yours.

3 **Why is it that a lot of guys I go with want to neck and pet all the time? Are they oversexed or am I just a prude? It seems all they're interested in is my body.** Or as one boy put it: **My girlfriend and I are engaged and seem to have a really good relationship. But I'm a bit worried about one problem. I seem to be much more interested in sex than she is.**

This is a common question and a big problem for many couples.

First, let me say that we scientists now find no real reason to believe that human males are any more highly sexed than females. Once she is aroused and ready for sex, the typical woman desires sex every bit as much as the man. But for at least four very good reasons, based on sex differences, most young men are much more interested in sex than young women of the same age. Some of these reasons are rooted in biological differences.

For one thing, a male's sex desires are usually much more quick to get aroused than female sex desires. That's why there are more "girlie" magazines than "boyie" magazines. Most women are left more or less unmoved by the near-nude picture of a male. (That may, of course, say something about the lack of beauty of the average male anatomy.) Most males, on the other hand, like to ogle pictures of females in sexy garb or suggestive positions.

One reason for this is biological. A male usually reaches puberty and is able to make a female pregnant at about age 11 to 13. From that point on his body keeps producing and storing up sexual fluids. Men produce about 50,000 live sperm every minute. These build up pressures that constantly remind him of sex. He is quick to notice the slightest thing related to sex—a girl in a short skirt or tight jeans, a low-cut blouse or a snug sweater may get him aroused.

But who ever heard of a girl getting antsy at a boy's tight sweater? Or even one with no shirt on at all? Most don't. Many don't even notice, much less feel sexy or get excited. That's because their sex desires are much slower to be aroused. Their bodies do not keep building up sexual fluids that cry out for release the same way men's bodies do. They are not constantly reminded of sex in this way.

Many women report that, unless sexually aroused by necking or petting, they may go for weeks or months and not give sex a second thought. Most men can't do that. Some men relieve this built-up pressure themselves. They masturbate. If they do not do so, nature will take care of it for them through a process we call nocturnal emissions. That's just a fancy name for wet dreams. Male fetuses even get erections while still in their mother's womb.[2] No wonder girls complain that boys are much too interested in sex. They are.

A third reason males seem more occupied with sex than females is that more of a man's sensitive sex organs are on the outside of his body. His clothes touch them or rub them when he walks. When he goes to the bathroom he must touch and hold his penis to guide the stream of urine. Females don't have that problem. They seldom need to touch themselves, except perhaps to wipe away excess urine or apply pads or tampons when they menstruate.

Finally, there is a wide gap between the time males and females (on the average) reach the peak of their sexual sensitivity. Males are most driven by their sex urges at about ages 17 to 19. Females don't reach their peak of sex interest until about age 28, or even their early 30s. Males peak late in high school or early in the college years—at the height of many men's courtship period. Females lag behind them by a full decade.

For these reasons many high school or college-age girls sometimes think they are out with a sex maniac. The guy seems to have more hands than a centipede has feet! The girl has to keep her guard up all the time. He seems to have foreign limbs: "Russian" hands and "Roman" fingers! And the guy may think he's out with a cold fish!

A footnote: Just because a guy feels more sexy at a given age is no excuse for him to be all hands or be rude to a girl. It's his problem, not hers. She has no obligation at all to let him touch her in ways she finds offensive. She has every right to tell him to bug off—or if he insists, to slap his sassy face. That can cool a pushy guy's ardor right fast.

4 **My fiancee seems much less interested in sex than I am. Is this a bad sign? Does this mean we won't have a good sex life after we marry? Should I break up with her before it's too late?**

It would be foolish to break up for that reason. I doubt that your worry is justified. For reasons just cited above, it is quite normal in our society for young single men to have a keener surface interest in sex than young women of the same age. Another factor, of course, is that women are the ones who get pregnant. They feel they simply *must* control the amount of their sexual expression, even if men refuse to do so. That's why most women tend to put on the brakes when they think things have gone far enough.

But once she is secure in a marriage, a woman can then release herself fully and freely in sex. She no longer needs to feel guilt or fear when she and her mate have sex. Once a couple have that piece of paper, our society, our parents, and our religion all say it's OK to have sex. In fact, they all just assume you will have sex when you wed. They'll think you're very odd if you do not. And you will be.

So you can't judge what kind of response a woman will have after marriage by the way she acts now. There is one good clue a couple has as to the kind of sex life they will have when wed. It is this: Do they have a *good overall relationship now?* How do they treat each other? If they are kind and thoughtful with the other now, they will likely be the same later. If they want to do things to please each other now, they will likely want to please each other in their sex life together. Selfish and mean now, selfish and mean later.

So don't worry about being able to work out a good future sex life after you get married. If two people really love and care about each other, their sex life will be just fine. They may have to do some good reading—perhaps get some counseling. But even if they do have to work at it, the results will be well worth it. In time they will be able to have a fine sex life.

5 If a boy always wants to talk about sex, does that mean he'll be a good sex partner?

Not at all. He may be all talk. Some guys think that if they talk about sex a lot it will make the girl want to have sex. It's just another "line" to get her into bed.

Or the locker room braggart may be making it all up just to appear macho. He wants to impress the other guys.

Nor is it a sign of good future sex in marriage just because a couple gets sexually excited when they neck or pet. Some girls, sadly enough, like to tease boys and get them aroused, and then not follow through. That could risk date rape. Or a person may get excited up to a point, but have all sorts of hangups when it comes to sex itself.

The best way to judge if a person will be a good sex mate is to watch closely *all* their behavior *before* marriage. One simple symptom is not enough.

6 Is there such a thing as having too much sex?

Yes, having too much sex can cause two problems.

First, having sex a lot of times in a short span of time can cause "sexual anesthesia." That is, there is a brief loss of feeling in the sex organs. This may occur with newlywed couples. Let's assume they have vowed to wait for sex until the wedding. That means they will likely be very eager to have sex. They may have it time after time on the honeymoon. In that case, the senses in their sex organs may grow dull for awhile. Sex then loses some of its appeal. (This may also happen to one who masturbates too often and/or too harshly.) But there is no problem. Full sensual feelings will come back very soon, and enjoyment of sex will be as good as ever.

Second, if a person has sex many times with many different people, sex stops being "special." It gets to be routine and "ho hum." Just like the person who has a steak dinner twice a day, week after week. Having steak is not all that great anymore. It may even grow tiresome.

So it is with sex. You can have "too much of a good thing." Sex can lose much of its zest. One boy told a research team that sex was no big deal for him. "Having sex with a girl means no more to me than shaking hands with her," he said.

WOW! Either that young man has one whale of a hand-shake, or he's missing out on a whole world of joys and pleasures that sex can and should be.

The ancient Greeks were smart enough to see this. They came up with the idea that too much of any one part of life, however pleasing, was not good. They called it the "golden mean." Life will be more full and worthwhile if one strikes a good balance. Joys of the mind, body, feelings, social life, and things of the spirit should be kept in proper balance. Not a bad idea, I'd say.

PART 2

About These Bodies of Ours

7 Why does a girl have to put up with menstruation?

If a girl ever wants to have a baby, menstruation just happens to be one part of the whole process. She's made that way. About once a month after she reaches puberty, one of her two egg-growing organs (called an ovary) sends out an egg or ovum. It travels down her oviducts, or Fallopian tubes, that lead to her uterus (womb).

Every time a woman ovulates, the ovary somehow sends a message down to the uterus or womb: "Get ready. Here comes an egg." (Well—maybe it's not *quite* that way!) Rather, the chemistry of her body lets her uterus know. The uterus then begins to collect blood-like (endometrial) tissue in its inner wall. If the egg is fertilized, this "zygote" attaches itself to the wall of the uterus. It is then fed by the congested tissue.

If the egg is not fertilized, it just dissolves. The collected matter in the uterus then serves no purpose. This lining is shed from the womb through the vagina in the form of menstrual flow.

This process continues month after month until a woman does get pregnant. Then she usually stops menstruating until several weeks after her child is born.

8 What is puberty?

It is the point at which a person becomes capable of being fertile. For the young girl it is when she begins to emit eggs from her ovaries and starts to menstruate. For the boy, it starts when he produces live sperm in his ejaculate.

9 Can a girl get pregnant before she starts to menstruate?

Yes, she can. Some girls have been known to have a baby before they have menstruated even once.

The reason is simple. One egg is released into her oviduct *before* she menstruates for the first time. If that egg is fertilized by a male sperm, then her very first menstrual period will not occur until after the baby comes. Instead, that stored tissue is used to feed the new little life in her womb.

In the same way, a woman may have two babies in a row without having a period in between. The very first egg released after the birth may be fertilized. The whole process is then repeated.

10 What does ejaculation mean?

When a male reaches a sexual peak of feeling, he usually has an ejaculation. That is, spurts of whitish matter called semen come out the end of his penis. Only a small part of the semen is actually live sperm. According to the new Kinsey report (1990), a male can ejaculate without having an orgasm, or orgasm without ejaculating.[1] (Frankly, I doubt that.) After the ejaculation he will almost always lose his erection.

11 What makes a man's penis hard?

That "hardness" is called an erection. It's caused simply by blood. It collects in his penis as the male gets more and more sexually excited. Amazing, isn't it?

12 What is the average depth of a woman's vagina?

The vagina is very flexible. It usually stretches over the penis with no problem in both depth and breadth.

13 How far does a penis penetrate into the vagina when a man and woman have intercourse?

That depends. The depth can be regulated by the use of different kinds of positions for intercourse. Each couple can make their own choice in that regard.

14 Can a girl get pregnant without having had sexual intercourse?

You bet she can. Each male sperm has a tail. It can swim. And every time a sperm gets into a warm, semi-liquid solution, it swims in all directions. Why? It wants to find the female egg or ovum. That's its sole goal: to get at that egg.

So here's a couple who have never gone all the way. But they do go pretty far down the road to arousal. In fact, they neck and pet so much that the male ejaculates (has a sexual discharge). That means there are between 100 million and 500 million "little men" on the loose. And every one of them wants to reach the egg.

Now, if they've been petting so much that he ejaculated, she's no doubt been breathing pretty hard herself. She is sexually aroused. When that happens, her sex organs, both inside and outside her body, become warm and moist. These are excellent conditions for sperm swimming.

36

So if any of these sperm are introduced to her vagina, or even to her vulva (that part which can be seen from the outside), guess what? These sperm swim actively in every direction, looking for an opening up to the egg. Is there one? You bet there is. The sperm can go right up the same opening where the menstrual flow comes out. They swim up through the vagina, in through the uterus, up the Fallopian tubes, and sure enough. Another virgin has conceived.

It can happen, by the way, even if the man does *not* ejaculate. Why? Because scientists have found that even the preseminal fluids that ooze out the end of a male's penis when he's sexually excited contain live sperm about 40 percent of the time.

A girl is likely to get pregnant without having sex more often than one might think. A social services director in a small city told me that she's now getting about one case a year. A girl may never have been penetrated in sex, but she will still be pregnant. As more young people pet to climax, pregnancy happens more often. Genital-to-genital petting or even mutual masturbation can therefore expose a couple to pregnancy. Fresh sperm can be transferred to the vulva by the fingers as well as by the penis.

However, the link must be direct. A very worried boy asked if he had exposed his girlfriend to pregnancy. It seems that as they kissed and held each other close, he ejaculated. It not only surprised, but embarrassed him. The fluids soaked through his pants, her dress and her underwear just below her waist. He was scared. Could she get pregnant from that?

No, not unless some of the fluid was transferred directly to her sex organs. As long as a strip of dry skin stood between the ejaculate and her vulva, the sperm could not swim across it. As the ejaculate dries up, the sperm will die.

15 Is it normal for a girl's breasts to be shaped oddly?

Quite normal. There is no special shape or size that breasts must or should be. Breast size varies widely between females and even in the same female. This is nothing to worry about. Size or shape of breasts will not affect your sex life or your ability to nurse your babies. Some men have the silly notion that big bosoms mean that a woman is more sexy. That is just not true. A girl with small breasts may be a lot stronger in her responses to sex than one with huge ones.

It is also fairly common that one breast may be much smaller than the other on the same girl. Again, no problem. It is not a defect. One young man I knew did not know this. When he found out his girlfriend had one breast much smaller than the other, he broke up with her. He thought she was a freak. In fact, as it turned out, she was far more responsive to sex in her marriage than most.

16 I have only one testicle. Does that mean I can't make my future wife pregnant?

Not at all. In fact, you may even be more able to impregnate her than if you had two. Since the main biological purpose of sex is to reproduce, our bodies are made in a way to try to assure pregnancy. There's a lot of "overkill." Men produce tens of millions of live sperm every day or so, yet only one will fertilize the ovum or female egg. The rest are "biological insurance." The theory seems to be: the more sperm, the better the chances for babies.

In the same way, a second testicle in a male is to enhance the chance that he'll be fertile. If one testicle is lost or goes bad, the other can do the job. In fact, the one that's left may be even more fertile than the two together. The body seems to make up for the loss.

Take the case of Jim. One of his testicles atrophied (died) when he was very young. But no sweat. He was as sexy as the next guy. And after marriage, he fathered six kids. In fact, he was so fertile that they had to be very careful

38

to keep from having more. He once complained that he had only to *look* at his wife to make her pregnant. (He was kidding, of course.)

If you have any doubts that you are able to produce healthy sperm, see a doctor. A simple lab test gives a sperm count.

In some men, a testicle stays up in the body. It does not descend into the scrotum, the sack that holds the testicles. So if you have only one testicle, see your doctor and get the story straight. Testicles need to be at lower than body temperature. That's why testicles are in the scrotum (sack) outside the body.

17 What does a low sperm count mean, and how does it affect the chance of pregnancy?

A sperm count is done in a medical lab. A fresh sample of a male's semen is placed under a high-powered microscope. Then the semen is examined to measure the number and activity of the sperm. If the sperm are too sparse and not very lively, that is a low sperm count. If the count is too low, the male may not be able to father a child.

18 Does it physically feel different for the male after a vasectomy?

No. The male can have sex and enjoy it as before. There is just no sperm in the semen. Actually sperm is only a small part of the semen, so its absence is scarcely noticed by a man.

19 What is an orgasm?

It is a peak of sexual pleasure. In men, there is almost always an ejaculation at the same time. In women there may be a discharge, but not often.

20 **How often do women have orgasms?**

That varies a great deal both between women and in the same woman. Only 30 percent—less than one-third—have orgasms regularly during intercourse. Some women just do not have orgasms at all, although in many cases that can be changed. Some women may have orgasms several times when they have sex.[2] All of these different responses are quite "normal" for each of these women. Each woman should just accept her own pattern and enjoy it instead of striving to achieve some other goal. That might actually impede her own sex life, not make it better.

Very few women will have an orgasm the first times they have sex. It will probably take a while.

21 **I've been circumcised. Will that affect my sex life after I marry?**

The folds of skin that cover the head of the male penis are called the foreskin. Circumcision is the surgical clipping away of that foreskin, usually when a boy is a very small baby. It became a religious ritual among Old Testament Jews and is still widely practiced by Jews and some Christians.

For most people today, circumcision—if it is practiced at all—is done for reasons of health, not religion. Since most small boys seem "allergic" to soap and water, they are not likely to wash with enough care under the foreskin when they bathe. Dirt and other impurities may collect there and cause irritation, infection, or disease. Therefore many doctors will suggest that male babies be circumcised.

As far as scientists can tell, there is no effect whatever on the sex life of such men. It will not make a man more sexy, or less so. Nor is the pleasure of sex in any way affected. It should be no cause for concern.

Some societies circumcise small girls by cutting out their clitoris. That robs them of sexual pleasure. It's a gross, barbaric practice.

22 **If a wife does not have a hymen, doesn't that mean she's had sex with some man before?**

Not at all. The hymen is a piece of flesh—usually quite thin—which may in part block the opening to the vagina. There is no sure-fire physical way to tell if a woman has had intercourse before. For one thing, some women are born without a hymen. (That caused no end of grief for such women in years past. Men would sometimes accuse their brides unfairly when there was no blood from a ruptured hymen on the wedding night.)

A hymen may be broken from other causes than by having sex. A girl may break it while masturbating, if in the process she inserts some object into the vagina. However, it is a myth that the hymen will be broken while playing tennis, or in gym class, or while riding a horse or bike. Such tales in the past probably arose as an excuse for women who had no hymen. Or for those who had lost it in a past sexual encounter.

On the other hand, even a woman *with* a hymen may well have had sex before. It could have just stretched over the penis without breaking. Or she may have stretched it enough while she masturbated to allow it to fit over the male penis and not be ruptured.

In most cases even doctors cannot tell if a woman has had intercourse before. True, some hymens simply could not have been unbroken if she had had sex. And in cases of forced rape, a doctor will likely be able to tell. But for the most part that is a secret only the woman herself can know for sure. Her husband will just have to trust her.

23 **Is there usually pain when you have sexual intercourse?**

Not usually. When there is a relaxed time of tender touching (called foreplay) before intercourse, there should be no pain. The sex organs are then well prepared so that

41

the penis enters the vagina with little or no resistance. There are three exceptions.

First, it may be painful if intercourse breaks the hymen.

Second, if the penis is forced in with little or no foreplay, there can be great pain for the woman. In cases of forced rape, the pain can be extremely severe. That's why rape is one of the most vicious of all crimes. Such an experience may leave deep mental scars on a woman that last long years after the act itself.

A lovely young mother told of being bound and brutally raped by three men for more than three hours. She was a virgin girl. She was beaten and forced to perform all kinds of sex acts repulsive to her. The pain was beyond description. Worse yet, she got pregnant and felt she had to submit to a tragic abortion.

Now, years after that nightmare experience, she is married to a fine man and has two children. Her husband is most gentle and understanding. Yet even so, she still "freezes up" with fear when he approaches her for sex. She in turn can't bring herself to make the first move toward him. And so their sex life has been greatly impaired.

She will no doubt need long sessions of counseling before she can, if ever, have a normal reaction to sex. What a terrible price she and her husband must pay for that one brutal incident for which she was in no way at fault.

This extreme case should make one thing crystal clear. *No man—married or not—ever has the right to press for his own sexual pleasure if the woman is feeling pain.* If he loves her, he most certainly will not wish to hurt her. That's one reason married sex is safer. There is mutual love and caring and sharing. There should be no desire whatever to bring pain to one's partner.

The third cause of pain can be one's attitudes and emotions. If the woman is afraid she'll get pregnant or fears there will be pain, her fear may actually bring on the pain. Her muscles spasm or tighten. Perhaps without knowing it, she is resisting sex. Some of the cause of pain in intercourse is brought on by the mind, not the body. Poor sex adjustment is rarely due to sex organ size or other physical causes.

24 What would you recommend a girl do when she is forced to have sex?

First, she should report the rape to a person she knows she can trust: a parent, a pastor, a counselor, a teacher. She should not just harbor those deep feelings inside herself. A woman can turn to rape or abuse centers in many communities in her time of need.

Then she should go with that trusted person to a hospital or medical clinic at once. She needs an examination and treatment for any damage done to her body. Some clues as to the identity of the rapist may be discovered. That also provides proof that she was indeed raped, in case she wishes to press charges later.

Next, and this may be hard to do. The person who did it—even if it was a member of her family, a boyfriend, or a family friend—deserves to be punished. And if she feels she can handle it, she should consider reporting the rapist to the abuse center staff or to the police. More and more rape victims are reporting the crime against them. This not only will, we hope, help punish the rapist for his violent act. It also may help keep him from doing the same thing again to her or some other women.

Rape must never be excused on the grounds that "boys will be boys." These "boys" must take full responsibility for their deeds, just like anyone else.

Finally, as in the case cited above, she will likely need to have good counseling, perhaps over a long period of time.

25 I've heard that first sex can hurt an awful lot. Is there some way I can keep that from happening?

Yes, for some women—but certainly not all—first intercourse may be quite painful. There are several ways to avoid such pain when you first have sex—hopefully on your wedding night.

In my view it is very foolish for a bride and groom these days to break the hymen on the marriage bed. Since it is no real test of her virginity anyway, it no longer serves a good purpose. In fact, it can cause lots of grief. It is a barbaric custom in my view.

For instance, here's a couple who have fiercely resisted the urge to have premarital sex. They are determined to wait for sex until married. As a result, they are of course going to be very eager to have sex very often once wed. They may even want it several times a day at first.

But what happens? When the hymen is broken, there will be an open wound. It will sting and hurt. Must they then wait several days for it to heal before having sex again? If they do not, each time they have intercourse the wound will just be reopened. Again and again there will be pain. This is scarcely the best way to start off a honeymoon. A couple can avert such a problem quite simply.

One answer is for the bride-to-be to have her doctor check her when she has her medical exam. In rare cases the hymen is so thick it can't possibly be broken in intercourse. If the hymen looks like it may be a problem, it can be solved with ease. In a simple surgical operation, a doctor can clip the hymen. It then has plenty of time to heal before the wedding.

The second method can be completed by the woman herself. A few weeks before the wedding she can begin to stretch the hymen. She can expand it little by little with her fingers so that it will stretch over the penis without pain when they first have sex.

26 **Do women reach another sexual peak at age 40?**

44

Probably not, unless she has an early menopause, commonly called a "change of life." Menopause is the time when women begin to lose their ability to ovulate or have a child. It used to occur about age 45. Now, a woman in the United States will have her last menstrual flow by the average age of 51.[3] Actual age varies with different women. A woman cannot be sure she can't get pregnant until two years have passed since her last menstruation.

PART 3

How Old Is Old Enough?

27 **What's a good age to start dating?**

As a rule, I doubt if it's wise for a girl to date one-to-one alone before age 16, or for a boy before 17. Before that, young folks of similar ages can have loads of fun going for cokes or pizza in mixed groups. Many won't even care to pair off at this stage. No need to rush into dating. Enjoy being young. Wait to date.

For one thing, studies show that the younger you are when you start to date, the more likely you are to get serious and go steady. Those who go steady younger are in turn the more likely to get involved more deeply in sex. They are also more likely to marry young. They may even *have* to get married. Half of all teenage women who now stand at the altar for marriage are already pregnant. And forced marriages, as well as young marriages, are far more likely to fail.

28 **How old should a person be to go steady with someone?**

For the above and other reasons, it is probably not a good idea to go steady in high school at all. Ask yourself: "Would I choose the same mate at age 25 that I would at age 17?" For most of us the answer would be a hefty *no!* For instance, in high school I felt sure I was in love. It never occurred to me that we would not get married. But thank heavens we did not. It would have been an absolute disaster. I doubt it would have lasted more than six months.

For one thing, if you home in on only one person too soon, how can you be sure you've made the best choice? As your relationship grows you may well wonder: "Is this really the one for me?" A good question. And how can you be sure if you haven't dated other people? You probably can't.

High school age is a time to go with a number of others. This helps you sort out the things you like and don't like in persons of the opposite sex. You learn from experience. You learn what to look for and what to avoid.

You may face two problems here. In some schools kids have the silly idea that if a couple goes out together more than once they are going steady. He's her guy, and she's his girl. So nobody else is supposed to intrude. That is sheer nonsense. If your school has any such stupid system, get a bunch of kids together and put a stop to it. You can do it if you just stick together and hold the line.

Another silly, even dangerous idea around some schools should be stopped dead in its tracks by the girls. Some people seem to think that if a girl dates around, going with first one and then another boy, that she must be "loose" or "on the prowl." What hogwash! She is just being smart.

The exact opposite is in fact true. The person who dates a variety of persons for only a few times each is far less likely to get into deep water with sex than the couple that goes steady. The longer the couple dates, the farther they're likely to go in sex.

So just because a girl has the good sense to seek variety in her dating does not mean she is "hot for sex." Girls should band together and stop such foolish nonsense.

29 What about age differences in dating?

That depends on what age you are, and which way the difference is. A high school senior girl who dates freshman boys will be in for a lot of flack and teasing. She will get ribbed for "robbing the cradle" or worse. Yet people think nothing of a senior boy dating freshman girls, even though the age spread is the same. That's because girls mature faster by about two years in almost every way. That led one young woman to ask . . .

30 Why are guys so immature?

A lot of girls wonder about that. A girl is usually ahead of most boys her own age. He may lag behind her in school performance. She may have developed more social skills. She reaches puberty first. She may be interested in boys before he cares one whit about girls.

In truth, both are quite normal for their age. Young men like to think they catch up to the girls later.

Still, the mid-teen or younger girl who dates a boy more than one or two years older may be in for some problems. Older, more experienced boys may press her to go farther in sex than she otherwise would or should. Since she feels flattered that an older boy is interested in her she may be tempted to "give in" to hold his interest.

Scientists call this the "principle of least interest." That is, the person who is less interested in having the relationship go on is in a position to call the shots. The more serious of the two will give in rather than risk a breakup. That could spell bad news.

It is even more of a danger if the boy is five or ten years older than the girl. In the teens it's much better to stick with kids roughly your own age. That's why most parents will object if there is much of an age gap.

However, it's less a problem once both the man and woman are fully mature. (Usually that means at least age 20 or more.) Why? Because scientists have found that even marriages with large age gaps of five, ten, or more years are just about as likely to succeed as marriages in general. The key seems to be maturity. Both need to be old enough and "grown-up" enough to know just what they're doing, and be willing to cope.

31 Why is it thought that the guy should be older than the girl?

The average age for a woman to marry in the United States now is just about 24 years. Males marry between 26 and 27. These ages are the highest since this century began. They represent an increase of three years for both men and women since the year 1975.

A number of reasons explain this age difference. One is tradition. Years ago, when a wife's role was confined to the home, it made sense. A girl could learn at a very young age how to cook and keep house and change a baby. Therefore she was able to fill her role as wife early on. The young man, on the other hand, had to take time to learn a trade or a skill so he could support a wife and children. That would take quite a few years. It was only natural that a woman would be more apt to marry a man somewhat older than she.

To some extent, this is still true. In spite of gains made in women's rights, husbands are still more likely to be the main money-maker. It is more and more difficult now to make a living without at least a high school, if not a college degree. That pushes back the time young men plan to marry.

And there are other factors. Remember: Girls tend to develop about two years ahead of boys in almost every way. That means that a girl's mind, body, spirit, emotions, and social life mature sooner. In the early years men lag behind. That is why many young women feel more at ease with men a bit older than themselves. Their ages may be different, but they may be more equal in maturity.

Also, more people are now living-in before marriage. That tends to postpone the age they wed.

32 What's the best age to marry?

If you want to play the odds, the longer you wait, the better. Marriages in the late 20s fail less often than those in the mid-20s. The mid-20s are better than the early 20s. And any time in the 20s is better than the teens.

However, the rate of failure is not the only thing to think about. The safest age for a woman to have babies, for instance, is in her 20s. As a rule, each year before 20—and especially under age 18—or after 31 that she gets pregnant, the more problems she will have.[1] There will be more danger to her own health and more risk for her child. She will face more risks of losing the baby and more hardships both in carrying and giving birth to her child. Her baby will be more likely to be born dead or deformed, or premature and underweight.

Other factors need to be weighed. When parents are too old, the "generation gap" in age between them and their children is greater. And after age 30, the chances that one will marry in the next calendar year will grow less and less. Many of the best mate choices are already wed.

All in all, a good balance may be best. Males might want to marry in their mid- or late 20s, females in their early to mid-20s. By then both should be able to assume all of the duties and privileges of marriage.

33 What is a good age for a person to start having sex?

The age when one *can* have sex and when one *has the right* to have it are two quite different things.

Even a small preschool child is able to have sex. Boys are able to have an erection at a very early age—long before they are able to have a male discharge (ejaculation).

In one sad case, a male in his teens had intercourse with a girl of five. In another case, two four-year-old children had sex as a form of play. (That is, they did until they got caught. Then their folks stopped letting them play together at all.)

Just because we *can* have sex at such an early age does not mean we have a *right* to do it. The main question is not one of age, but of situation. Some girls are able to have a baby at age 11. One case is reported of a girl in South America getting pregnant at age four.[2] But does that mean that these children *should* have sex and have a baby just because they *can*?

Boys in turn can get a girl pregnant at age 12—and maybe at 11 or even 10. Does that mean that they are capable of being a good father and husband at that tender age?

Let's pause to mention some of the dire risks involved in getting into sex at an early age. The younger the girl is when she starts having sex, the earlier she will get pregnant and have a baby. And the earlier she will marry. And the more likely that her first sexual encounter was not her choice. She was forced.[3] Girls who had sex before age 14 are especially at risk.

At what age then, does one have a right to have sex? Not until he or she is able to take full responsibility for the results of that sex. In our society, that means not until you are married. No couple has the right to have sex until they are old enough and grown-up enough to support themselves and care for any children they might have. What does that mean? Well, as of now there is absolutely no 100 percent way to avoid the risk of getting pregnant or getting AIDS or other STDs. That means that unless you are willing to become a parent RIGHT NOW! THIS VERY MINUTE!, you have no right to enjoy the pleasures of having sex. In fact, that means that it is not at all smart to engage in sex until you are married.

PART 4

Dating Not for Mating

34 How can I attract someone of the opposite sex? I'm not very pretty. How can I get someone I like to like me?

That may not be easy. If you happen to be one whose face and figure are very attractive, it's not so rough. But most of us wouldn't win any beauty contests. It's too bad that some people put so much stock in the outward looks of others, but they do.

Perhaps the prayer of Reinhold Niebuhr may be a good thing to keep in mind here:

> God, give us grace to accept with serenity the things that cannot be changed, courage to change the things which should be changed, and the wisdom to distinguish the one from the other.

Most of us can't do much about the face or figure we have been given. We can't do much about the size of our body and—short of plastic surgery—the shape of our nose or face. We can't help it if we have an overbite or a flat chest. We just have to accept what we cannot change.

But there are many things we *can* change. We can go on a diet if we are too fat. We can change our disposition and our attitudes. We can get into the habit of being cheerful instead of grumpy. We can try always to be pleasant and friendly. We can give others sincere compliments and encouragement rather than criticisms and put-downs. No one likes to be around a grump or a gripe, or a snob or a snitch. We like people who are pleasant and happy and nice, who have a sense of humor, and who respect and like other people as well as themselves.

These are things we *can* change. So instead of going around moping and moaning about what we cannot change, why not focus on the things we can? Let a smile be your trademark. Not a false, silly grin—everyone will soon catch on to that—but an honest, open, caring, friendly smile. A genuine, pleasant smile when you meet another says to that person: "I want to be friends. How about you?"

Be on the lookout for things you can like and admire about others. Watch for ways you can give them a sincere pat on the back. All of us like to be appreciated, and we like the people who do the appreciating.

There's an old saying that goes, "Pretty is as pretty does." A girl can be pretty to look at, but still be a spoiled brat. But pretty (or handsome) or not, we can all become beautiful people. Isn't that the more important thing?

35 How can I know if he (or she) really likes me?

That depends a lot on what age the person is. At junior high age or younger, we tend to treat the girl (or boy) we like in very strange ways. A boy may throw snowballs at the girl he likes best. He may pull her hair or "show off" around her by chinning himself on the monkey bars. Or he may race around faster than anyone else—when he thinks she's watching. He may tease her a lot.

A girl may pretend she's just chatting with girl friends. But she may exaggerate her facial expressions or her hand gestures—all the while casting shy, sly glances at a boy to see if he's noticed her. Yet she may act like he's not alive when she meets him alone on the street. That's because she may not know quite how to act. She may be too shy and embarrassed even to be pleasant and friendly. Neither a boy nor a girl at this age wants to appear too obvious or to let on that they like the other person. They play-act a lot. They try to give hints that they are interested without really saying so.

By high school age, young men and women are feeling more secure and self-assured. They gradually become less afraid to let the other person know how they feel. They are more likely to admit openly to themselves and to others that they think the other is pretty nice. They may stop and chat in the hall between classes. A boy may walk a girl home from school. They may "happen" to meet at the lunch table or water fountain—not really by chance, of course. They may flirt a lot. But they may still play games.

As young people get older and more mature, they are less likely to play such games with each other. They feel more free to show openly that they like the other person. If they'd like to know someone better or to go out, they will probably come right out and admit it. A boy will ask a girl out, or she will find ways to let him know that she would be pleased if he showed her more attention. As friendship grows, they may be able to tell each other just how they feel.

Frankly, I'm a great believer in being honest and open in dating and courtship relationships. Mature young people don't need to play cat-and-mouse games. If you like someone, why keep it a secret? And by the same token, if you don't care for someone who keeps showing interest in you, why put off telling them the truth? If a girl doesn't like a certain guy, she shouldn't keep him in the dark. Be frank and honest, but be kind. Don't say to your sister or roommate, "If Bill calls, tell him I'm not home!" or "Gosh! There's Suzie down the hall. Let's go this way so she won't see me!"

36 What is a good thing to say to a girl when you first meet her?

Talk about something you share in common. If you have a class in school together, talk about that tough test you just had. Or you might be a little sneaky and ask about the next assignment—even though you know what it is already. If you are in the same church youth group, talk about that. Anything to break the ice. Just be yourself and see how it goes.

37 If you think you like someone but aren't sure they like you in return, should you risk asking them out?

Why not? The worst thing that can happen is for them to say no. Nothing ventured, nothing gained. A girl may be wise to be a bit cautious in asking for that first date. Be sure he's "liberated" and won't be turned off. Otherwise, go for it.

38 There is this guy that I really like. But he only seems to care about me when he is not around or near his friends. Why is this and what can be done about it?

Some guys, mainly younger ones, are weird that way. They're between a rock and a hard place. On the one hand, he may like a girl and like to be around her when his friends can't see him. But when they are in sight, he knows they'll give him a hard time. They'll tease him if he pays attention to her. As he gets older, he may not care. His friends are likely to like girls, too.

Of course, there's also a chance that he's ashamed to be seen with her. If that's the case, she should probably dump him fast. He's not worth her time.

39 Is it OK to be friends first, and then go out with someone?

By all means. Relationships built on friendship are the best kind. I wouldn't even think of getting serious about someone you could not be real friends with. The person you marry should be a best friend.

40 Is it right to date others before marriage, even if the people dating don't intend to marry?

By all means. How else can you get to know what you like and don't like about persons of the other sex? That is likely the best chance you will ever have to date a wide variety of fine young people found in every school. It's the best way to prepare for choosing a mate wisely, once you do decide to settle down with one person for the long pull.

Further, it's quite OK to date someone just because they are fun to be with. You don't need to have romantic feelings. Fun is fine—if it doesn't spoil something better.

41 When you like a girl a lot, and you find out she does not like you, should you try to make her like you or go on with your life?

If you are very sure that she does not like you, you'd be wise to look elsewhere. To pursue her too much right now will likely just drive her farther away. If at some future time the person changes her/his mind, you will have time then to work something out. But as of now, get on with your life and try not to let it bother you too much. Remember the old saying, "There are bigger and better fish in the sea than have ever been caught out." Keep your hooks baited! Just don't catch any suckers.

42 Is it old-fashioned if you don't want to kiss on the first date?

Not at all. You do not need to feel you have to kiss anyone at *any* time if you don't really want to. For one thing, a kiss or any other expression of affection does not mean much unless it is given freely. And then only when you really mean it. Also, if word gets around that you kiss (or make out) on the first date, you'll get tagged as an easy mark. Your kisses lose their value if you toss them around like chicken feed. And think of all those germs you'll get!

A beloved old teacher at Willamette University used to talk to each new class of women. "Advice to the freshman girl," he would say with a kindly smile. "You have only one kiss to give. Bestow it wisely."

Well said. Gestures of caring should mean something important, both to the one who gives and the one who receives. Better to be sincere and honest, to live one's own life. Never mind what others say. Never mind what the couple is doing in the back seat of the car. They may do that in the back seat and not get AIDS or pregnant. You may do it in the front seat and get both! Do what *you* think is right, not what others want or expect you to do.

Some girls think they owe a boy some favors in return for taking them on a date. That is just not so. The pleasure of being with you is all a guy has a right to expect. If he expects more and gets ticked off if he doesn't get it, that should be a tip-off. Ask yourself, "Does this guy like me as a person and want to be with me for myself? Or does he go with me for my body or for what favors or kicks he can get out of me?" If it's the latter, then he's using you. That isn't flattering, is it? The only kiss you ought to give such a guy is the kiss-*off!* Tell him to get lost. And good riddance.

43 **I spend quite a lot of bucks on girls when I take them out. I have a nice car and we go to eat, or to a movie, or we bowl or whatever. I sometimes think girls go with me just for the things I buy for them. Could that be true?**

You bet it could. Some girls use boys to get what they want every bit as much as some boys use girls for the sex thrills they might get. Boys have no corner on the art of taking advantage of the other sex.

But that doesn't make it right, does it? Just ask yourself, "Do *I* like it when I feel that someone is just using *me?*" Most of us don't like it. It makes us feel like a thing, not a person. It is a real put-down. Do we have any right to do the same to others?

Philosopher Immanuel Kant said we should always act toward others in such a way that we would be willing to have our act become a universal law. That is, we'd be willing to have everyone else behave in the very same way. Does that sound strangely like the golden rule, "Do unto others as you would have them do unto you?" Almost every major living religion has come up with that same idea. There just may be something to it!

44 When a boy comes over, what do you do besides make out and watch TV?

Surely you can come up with more things to do than that. If you don't, you may be in deep trouble. The "making out" can mean anything from holding hands and a hug to going all the way in sex. If all you do is make out every time you see each other, you may find yourself slipping farther and farther down "the road to arousal." And a little TV may go a long way. Much of the programming on the tube is shallow, violent, or raunchy. It wears thin mighty fast.

There are dozens of things a couple can do to enjoy an evening together. With a little advance planning, you can come up with good ideas. What do you both like to talk about? What games do you know, or could learn to play? How about making popcorn or candy or pizza instead of making out?

Why not involve others in your family—in discussions, games, etc.? Many parents and siblings would be pleased to be included if you would just invite them. They also may have a few suggestions of things you two might like to do. If you use your head for something more than a hat rack, I'm sure you can come up with a good list. If not, either one of two things is likely true. You two may have so little in common that your relationship will—and should—wither and die. Or you're not using your imagination and that fertile brain of yours.

45 Do guys like it when a girl openly flirts with them?

That depends. If a boy likes a girl, he may be thrilled or even flattered if she flirts with him. If not, it may embarrass him and turn him off. It depends on the guy and the occasion. He may like a girl and secretly enjoy the flirting when he's alone, but not like it when he's with other guys. They may tease him later. So he may pretend to them that he resents your attention. He may even treat you rudely in order to "save face" with his friends.

So if you feel like flirting, be cautious at first. Watch carefully how the guy takes it. If you sense a problem, back off. And be selective. Flirt only with those you really like. If you flirt with every Tom, Dick, and Harry, none of them will feel special. And you might get a bad reputation for your trouble.

46 Is it all right for a girl to ask a guy to go out?

Probably. It will depend on the guy and the situation. If it is an event where the women get to do all the asking, like a Sadie Hawkins Dance, then it's OK. Just explain that to him. If he turns you down, that's OK too. It will help you know how a guy feels when a girl turns *him* down!

But these days most young people aren't so fussy about what's been "correct" in the past.

Here's an interesting fact. Women tend to use more good sense when they choose men than men use in the choice of women. Studies show that men put much more weight on shallow things like good looks and a nice figure. Women are more apt to stress more important things. Is a man kind, considerate, and thoughtful? In this sense, then, women may do a better job of picking out dates than men!

47 What is the best way to handle money when on a date?

Alas, tradition still rears its ugly head and often triumphs over logic. In the past, men have always been the ones to ask and to pay. Many still feel that's the way it ought to be. A guy who feels that way may be turned off, not on, by a woman who is bold enough to ask him out. Some may even think she's on the loose side, "on the make" for sex.

Therefore a smart woman may wait until she knows a guy well enough to be quite sure what his response will be. Otherwise, she takes some risks.

Some shy guy may be glad the girl broke the ice and made the first move. Other guys may be scared off.

Age is also a factor here. Men who are college-age or older may be less likely to resent a woman who takes the initiative. Younger, less secure men are more prone to be repelled.

If you want to get to know a certain male better but don't want to risk offending him, try this: Don't ask him out alone, one-to-one, on a date. Pick a time when a group of you are going for pizza or burgers and ask him if he'd like to come, too. Then the scene shifts from you asking him to be with *you* to you inviting him to join the party. If he takes that in stride, you can judge whether or not to take the next step.

There is one further point. A fully liberated woman may use this means as a test to find out if a man shares her views on equality of sexes. It's like testing the water with your toe before plunging in.

So let's suppose a couple has an understanding on this score. They agree there will be no hard feelings if she asks for or pays for the date. Actually that makes some sense. Why should they both stay home just because he's broke, if she has the money for a dinner for two or a movie? If there's concern about what others might think if she pays, she can just slip him the money beforehand and let him do the honors.

48 Is everyone capable of loving?

Yes, all of us are. In rare cases persons may have such serious hangups that they seem unable to release love in the ways that will make them good marriage mates. They may be too selfish. They may be afraid of others. They may be full of hate and resentments.

But this type of plight is indeed rare. You are not likely to be in such a fix.

In any case, all of us can grow to love more and more. We can learn to look for ways we can help others. We can train ourselves to care about the needs of other people as well as our own. We can make it a habit to treat others as we would want to be treated if we were in their place. An old Indian proverb suggests, "If you would know another, walk in his (or her) moccasins for one week." Even one *day* would help.

It might help to play a game with yourself. Every time you see other people, try to figure out what their needs are. Then think how you can help them meet their needs (without, of course, going against your own moral or religious standards). It can be a fun game. And useful.

If you truly feel you are not now able to love, then see someone who is trained as a counselor. Some of the clergy or some school counselors are so trained. At least they can point to where you can get help.

49 **What about the saying, "opposites attract"?**

Opposites may attract, but are they likely to *stay* attracted? That innocent, sweet, young farm girl from Podunk Prairie may feel flattered by the attentions of some cool, dashing, self-assured city smoothie. But will her quiet rural feet feel at home when set down in the buzz and bustle of the big city? Will he come to resent her sweet, simple, unspoiled lack of urban skills in the presence of his city friends and family? Those who are quite different in their lifestyles, their hopes, their roots and religions, their roles and goals, do not often make good mates for the long pull. When the newness wears off, they will find little in common to hold their lives together.

In some cases, those who have opposite personal traits may be happy if they fill a need in each other. A shy type may admire and need a mate who is outgoing. They get a kind of mutual joy from the change of pace. Those who like to be bossy may get on well with those who like being bossed. But watch out if the bossed ones ever decide they've had enough. Then the sparks will fly!

As a rule, though, likes like likes longer than unlikes like unlikes. (Say that fast three times!) The more things a couple share in common, the better will be their chances for wedded bliss. Those who like the same things, go to the same church, enjoy the same friends, like each other's families, and agree on goals are far more likely to stay wed for keeps. The more things you like about each other and like to do together, the better.

50 **Why do guys use girls for sex objects?**

Not all guys do. Some boys do see girls mainly as a way to satisfy their sex urges. That's too bad.

But more and more it is not just guys who use girls. Boys now complain that some of the girls are coming on to them for sex. That's really foolish, since the girl is the one who can get pregnant. The girl is also more likely to catch an STD like AIDS than the boy. But foolish or not, boys say it is happening.

And where are young women getting such an idea? From the TV and some movies. Have you noticed? Now it's the girl who almost drags the guy into the bedroom and rapes him? He's portrayed—and this is most unreal—as the reluctant one who finally submits to her wiles. And it's the woman who is portrayed as having all the wild, ecstatic responses to that sex. Girls who don't know any better may buy into that nonsense.

Some boys now worry that if a boy refuses her advances, he may be accused of not being a real man. Actually, the guy's a hero, not a nerd. It takes real guts to turn down an invitation to have sex, especially at his age.

51 Why do guys always pressure you to have sex?

Some guys do test to the limit every girl they go out with. They see it as a challenge. They want to see just how far a girl will let them go. Each exploit is to them a victory. If he gets her to go all the way he is beside himself with pride. It's kind of like the gunfighters of the old West. Each man they killed, they'd put another notch on the handle of their six-guns.

But let me warn you, girls. Guys like that will usually "kiss and tell." They may even kiss and brag to the other envious guys. Then the girl gets the label as an easy mark. If so, all the boys are drawn to her like a cub bear to a honey tree. Every other guy she goes with will expect the same favors. It will be hard for her to regain her self-respect, if indeed she ever can.

52 How do you stop a guy from going too far?

Before you even go out on your first date, decide just where your limit is going to be on the road to arousal. Perhaps you will not even want to do any necking at first. When he tries to go beyond your limit, tell him in no uncertain terms that he can go only that far and no farther. Make it perfectly clear to him that "no" means "NO"—not maybe. Most boys will heed the warning.

Always carry some change with you on a date in case you have to call home. And don't let a guy take you out to a remote spot to park where the nearest phone is miles away, in case you have to walk home. Of course, after you've gone with the guy long enough to know he can be trusted, these precautions may not be needed.

If a guy continues to pester or try to abuse you, insist that he take you right home. Tell him if he doesn't, you will report him to his folks or in extreme cases to the authorities. If nothing else works, get out and phone home, or start to walk back. Better to have a little hike than have a little tyke!

53 What does a guy think of a girl when she lets him do almost anything he wants to because it doesn't bother her?

For one thing, she may get a reputation for having loose morals if or when the word gets around. At least I'm glad she only lets him do ALMOST anything he wants to.

This girl may be tempting trouble. Sometime she may go with a guy who gets so excited that he refuses to stop at "almost." She may be a victim of date rape, a tragedy now being reported more often.

On the other hand, she may be a victim of her own claim that it does not bother her. She may someday date a male who is very experienced in matters of sex. If he gets his hand on her vulva, she may lose control. If he knows what to touch and how to touch it he may drive her up the wall.

I fear this girl is skating on very thin ice. And if she falls through, the water is icy cold. Ask any girl who did.

54 **Why do guys think that they can just take advantage of a girl and think that it doesn't hurt her? I want every guy to think that over.**

You said it beautifully. I hope all the guys who are guilty of that will listen up.

Of course, girls can be guilty of the same kind of mistreatment of boys. In either case it is hard to forgive such actions.

PART 5

"Just You and Me, Sweetheart"

55 **You have said (in *Sex, Love, or Infatuation*) that each of us averages about nine or ten romantic experiences in our lifetime. How many of these are false love?**

About eight or nine of these will likely be puppy loves or infatuations. No more than one or two of them are likely to be real love.

Most persons who have found real love tend to think that all of their former romances were mere infatuations. They are probably right, too. But just try to convince them of that while the romance was going on! They'd likely have sworn up and down that they were really in love.

A gentle word of warning is in order here. No matter how much teenagers are "just sure" they are in love, they almost never are. Chances are extremely slim that adolescents have real love. I know it is very hard for you to believe that fact, especially when you get those stars in your eyes. But it is true. To check it out, consult the next chapter on "How Can I Know When It's Love." Better yet, get a copy of my book *Sex, Love, or Infatuation: How Can I Really Know?*[1] It will give you the right answer. Meanwhile, don't make any big decisions about your romance.

56 Why do girls fall in love more than guys?

It is true that girls tend to take their relationships more seriously than most boys. Part of that may be due to maternal instinct. (Males don't have much of that!) And again, it's partly because women mature quicker. For whatever reason, girls are in fact more likely to get serious. That means she has to be—even more than guys—more careful not to fool herself into thinking it is love and not a mere romance.

57 How can you assure your boyfriend that you love him and do not want anyone else?

If he won't take your word for it, that means he does not really trust you to tell the truth. Not a good sign. Be sure you do not do things to make him jealous. That will help.

Whatever you do, don't fall into the trap of "proving your love" by giving him sex. Real love doesn't have to be proved. If you are being truthful with him and he still won't believe you, that's his problem, not yours. But if he doesn't shape up soon, it will more and more be a problem for you, too. In that case you may wish to consider backing away.

58 How do I get over the jealousy I feel when my girlfriend is with other people?

Jealousy can mean many things. You may feel that you can't trust her. Or she may in fact not be trustworthy. You may feel a lack of self-worth and that you don't deserve her. This may lead to fear of losing her. You feel insecure and anxious. For whatever reason, jealous feelings can make a person feel terrible.

You don't say how involved you are with each other. If a couple get very much into sex, both will almost always get quite jealous. Why? Because you can't help but wonder: If he/she will do that with me, would they do it with others if they had half a chance? A good question. And too often it is true.

Studies show that those who go all the way with one person they date are far more likely to do the same later with others. Or if they have gone a certain distance down the road to arousal, they tend to move quite rapidly to that same level with their future partners. It's no wonder that couples who get very much into sex will almost always be jealous and suspicious.

59 What if your best friend doesn't like your girlfriend? He feels like you are not spending enough time with him.

This happens a lot. You've been close to each other, and suddenly you have other calls on your time. He feels neglected, and probably is. He is jealous of your girl. That's likely the reason why he does not like her. There's not a lot you can do about that, unless you and your girl break up. Other than that, your friend will just have to get used to the new situation. He has to realize that's just the way the dating ball bounces.

60 If a guy says he loves you, dumps you, but comes back feeling he made a mistake, asks for you back, do you feel it is probably love?

Most probably not love at all. I'd be really reluctant to take the guy back. He obviously doesn't know what he wants at this point. If he dumped you once, he may well do it again. But if you do go back to him, don't let him have sex. That may be what he hopes to get. It is pretty clear to me that the guy does not know what love is. I think I'd look for greener pastures.

61 We keep breaking up, and he keeps coming back to me. He has more infatuation for me than love. I have more love than infatuation. Will our relationship work?

Don't count on it. A one-sided love—if indeed that's what you really have for him—will not last. Love cannot be a one-way street. Love must be shared.

More than that, your many break-ups are a clue that your chances to make it together are very poor. Marriage scientists know that if a couple break up and get back together more than once, it's a red warning flag. Why? Because if that happens several times before the wedding bells ring, you can just bet it will go right on doing so after the romance and sex begin to fade.

Such couples can't stand to be apart, yet can't stand to stay together. They almost always end up hurting each other over and over, then finally calling it quits. Better to have the hurt of a rift now than more misery and a final bust later, don't you think?

62 Is it all right to go out with your brother's best friend?

Of course. If you and your brother get along well with each other, then the best friend he has chosen will likely be a good bet for you. You'd have a lot of things in common.

But if you were to go out with the best friend of your boyfriend, now that's quite a different story. It would likely lead to a double bust: between you and your boyfriend, and between him and his former best friend.

63 Is it wrong to have feelings for both your boyfriend and his brother?

It may not be wrong, but it certainly is dangerous. One—if not both—of them may get plenty jealous if you seem too fond of both at the same time. One result may be to cause problems between you and your friend. But it may also drive a deep wedge between the two boys and cause ill will in the family, as well as toward you.

As a young man I was very close friends with two sets of sisters. I was going with one of the four, but all five of us often went places together. All went well until I tried to date some of the others, too. That led to big trouble. All four got on my back fast.

If you want to stay healthy, better keep it one at a time.

64 If, after going out for a year, your boyfriend cheats on you with a younger girl but you still love him, is it love or infatuation?

Probably neither. He obviously does not love you or he would not have betrayed you like that. You may have strong emotional feelings for him, but that does not mean it is love.

Better run like a scared rabbit—away from this cad. If he cheated once, he'll probably do it again. Studies show that if people cheat before marriage, they will do so after. You can get along without that, for sure.

And another thing. The person who cheats on a partner runs a high risk of bringing home an STD and even AIDS. That's not just being unfaithful, it's being downright dangerous. Surely you don't want to take that kind of risk.

65 Is there an easy way to tell the person you're going with to get lost?

I doubt there is an easy way to end a romance. But some ways seem better than others.

Just out of the blue to blurt out, "Bug off, Buster!" or "Get lost, Lucy!" hardly seems the wise way to go. That's pretty crude and cruel, especially if it's done when others are around to hear you.

Keep two things in mind. First, as soon as you feel sure you no longer want the relationship to go on, say so. You owe it to the person and to yourself to tell the truth. That's only fair. It's not easy, but you do the other no favor by pretending you still care when you don't. The bitter pill will be just as hard to choke down tomorrow as it is today. Don't put it off.

But while you need to be fully frank, don't be brutally blunt. No need to club them over the head with the bad news. No hurt is more painful than a broken heart. A broken arm hurts only in that arm. A broken heart hurts all over. So be kind. Be gentle. Try to put the truth in ways that will ease the hurt. Don't do it in anger or in spite. That's a put-down. Do it instead in a quiet, matter-of-fact way that lets the person save face. If you can, try to keep the person as a friend.

66 What is a good way to let a friend know that sex should not be necessary for a lasting relationship?

Try giving them a few facts. Sex is important; it is not *all* important. No matter how good their sex is, it will hold a couple together no more than three to five years—and probably not that long. Also, the sex may blind them to the real nature of their relationship. It muddies the water. It fools them into thinking they have more going for them than they really have. And it tends to break couples up, since they often fight about it.

67 What is the best way to talk to your boy/girl friend about where to draw the line?

Why not pick a quiet time together when you are not doing any physical expression of your affection? Then simply explain how you feel. Give the main reasons why you want to set a particular limit. Say that you hope he or she will respect your decision. Then hold your ground. Don't budge unless you feel comfortable with some compromise you can agree on. And bully for you!

68 How long should you go together before you get married?

The general rule is, the longer the better. Those who go together the longest, stay married the longest. And they are happier, too.

Since the risks of a marriage failure are now so high, the smart thing to do is to take lots and lots of time. Err on the side of too much time rather than too little—if you err at all.

Remember, couples who take a full year to get to know each other better are on much sounder ground than those who wed after only six months. Two years of courtship and engagement are even safer, and three are better yet. And so are four and five. The more time you take to get to know the person well *before* you marry, the fewer surprises you'll have *after* you marry. Pick a reasonable amount of time, of course. (These 25-year engagements make no sense!)

Since marriage is now so risky, I think no couple should enter the high privilege of marriage—and I do see it as a high privilege—unless they've had at least two full years of courtship and engagement.

69 What does it mean to "flunk the test of time"?

The thrills of sex may hold a couple together for up to three to five years. So even if a couple date two years before they marry, they could still flunk the test. The pull back to each other for sex may fool them into thinking they have more in common than they do. To be sure you have passed the test of time, you need at least two years without the thrills of mutually satisfying sex. That's a bitter pill, but it needs to be swallowed if you want to avoid a poor marriage or divorce.

70 Are long engagements a good thing?

Yes, if you want to play the odds. Longer engagements more often lead to lasting, happy marriages.

The main thing here is to get to know the other person *really well* before you marry. The *total length* of time you take is the key. Whether you take that time in courtship or in engagement is not the most important thing. You can slice the pie of total time in any way you choose.

My own choice is a long courtship, but short engagement. When a couple gets engaged, they "go public." We assume that they have already decided that their relationship is a sound one. They just announce that they intend to go to the altar.

So no couple should get engaged until they feel quite sure it will be for keeps. For one thing, it may save them a lot of hassle. One out of every three engaged couples will break up before they get married. If a breakup comes after going public with a picture and story in the local press, you may feel pretty silly. It's even worse if the wedding announcements have already hit the mail. That makes for a lot of red faces. Best to avoid such a mess if you can.

71 Do you think that a long courtship can get you in trouble sexually?

It can. Studies show that engaged couples are much more likely to get more involved with sex after they're engaged. And they're more likely to go all the way. So if a couple wants to wait for sex until after they're wed, it will be easier to do so during a short engagement. At best, it is plenty tough these days for a couple to wait. No need to make it any harder than need be.

Therefore a lengthy courtship and a brief engagement seem best. Of course you should allow enough time so that the wedding plans can be made calmly and be carried out without too much stress. You don't want to faint at the altar from sheer exhaustion.

72 What about the couple who say: "We're engaged and the wedding is only a couple of months from now. Why should we wait any longer for sex?"

If you have stuck it out all this time, why not "go all the way"—not in sex, but in abstinence? This would be an achievement you two could really be proud of for years to come. In spite of everything, you reached that cherished goal you had set for yourselves those many months ago! What a great feeling that would be. And you could honestly tell your children about it, as an example you hope they would follow.

PART 6

Going It Alone: What about Masturbation?

73 What is masturbation?

Masturbation is touching or rubbing one's own sex organs for pleasure. A person may or may not reach a sexual climax (called an *orgasm*) in the process. This brings a peak of pleasure when it happens. A male orgasm is called an ejaculation, since spurts of sexual fluids called *semen* will come from the end of the erect penis.

Some females who masturbate touch their breasts as well as their vulva—the outer parts of their pelvic sex organs. Some also insert their fingers or other objects into their vagina.

74 How often do average people masturbate?

That depends on a lot of things. Most married people seldom masturbate, if at all. They have intercourse instead. This may change if they are absent from their spouse for a long time, if they are having problems in their relationship, or if their spouse is ill.

For a number of reasons men tend to masturbate much more often than women. One reason is that most are not married or living-in at the time they are at their peak of sexual interest—at ages 17 to 19. By age 28–35, when women reach their peak of interest, most women are married. I've already mentioned some other reasons why male sex interest is normally more quick to be aroused.

Another point is that a male will get an erection about once every 90 minutes while he is sleeping.[1] If he wakes up with one, he is much more likely to go ahead and masturbate. In any case, scientists have found that about 94 percent of all males masturbate quite regularly before they marry, unless they are sexually active. By contrast, only about 63 to 82 percent of females masturbate *at some time* before they marry.[2]

75 Do scientists think masturbating is wrong?

As of now, I know of no scientific evidence that masturbation will harm a person. It does not seem to affect the body, mind, nerves, or emotions.

There are a lot of myths about this subject, though. We were once told that doing it would make you go blind, or that it would drive you crazy. A high school classmate of mine hanged himself naked in his garage. A neighbor girl was asked why he did it. "Oh, he masturbated and it drove him out of his mind," she said. (How she knew that, she did not explain.)

Such claims are nonsense. Masturbation does not affect one's mind, with one exception: if you worry about it. Like any other worry, it can affect your mental health.

As a youth I was told that masturbation would make one's face break out in pimples. It won't. When an adolescent's body chemistry changes, it is quite normal for the face to have blemishes. But there was always some nosy neighborhood gossip who would watch the faces of teenagers. If she saw one who had such blemishes she'd raise an eyebrow. "I know what you're doing," she'd seem to say. Well, she may have been right. But the masturbation had nothing to do with the pimples.

Nor is masturbating "self-abuse." In no way does it abuse or do damage to a person. Another myth is that if you masturbate while single it will ruin your sex life after you're wed. It won't. Once you engage in full intercourse with your mate, you may forget all about masturbating. Why settle for hamburger when you can have steak?

All these myths were scare tactics to keep the young people from masturbating. But as of now, science has found no harmful results, unless the person worries about it.

Two minor cautions might be in order, however. If a girl inserts any object into her vagina, it could cause infection. Or if a person masturbates too often or too much at one time, it may cause some temporary loss of feeling in the sex organs.

76 Can you turn gay after you masturbate?

I know of no evidence at all that supports this view. We just don't know yet what makes a person come to prefer others of the same sex. Some people think it's brought on due to certain kinds of relations with parents or siblings. Some think the tendency may be inherited. Some say it is learned as a child through group masturbation, or masturbating another person, or oral or other sex experiments. We just don't know. Frankly, I doubt that masturbation is a factor at all. I suspect that it takes far more than masturbation to lead a man into being gay or to make a woman into a lesbian.

We do know that once people have the chance for intercourse with a mate, the need to masturbate is largely lost.

77 Can you get AIDS from masturbating?

Not at all. AIDS (Acquired Immunodeficiency Syndrome) is only spread from person to person. Unless you do something to expose yourself to the HIV virus, you won't get AIDS. You can be exposed by having vaginal, anal, or possibly oral sex with a person who is infected. Or using a needle to shoot drugs or steroids after an infected person used it. But you can't get it by masturbating yourself.

78 If you masturbate and get fresh sperm on your hands and put it in the vagina, can she get pregnant?

That is possible. Any time fresh live sperm have access to the vagina, a mature female can conceive. Better not to mess around like that.

79 Is masturbation a sin?

If it makes you feel guilty when you do it, then it is a sin for you. Sin means missing the mark. If you fall short of what you feel you ought to do, then you sin in your own eyes.

But you can sin even if you do not feel guilty. Guilt is learned, so it can be unlearned. People who steal over and over soon feel little or no guilt when they do it. Yet it is still a sin since it is hurting someone else. It is also falling short of what you could do or be. That is not right. For religious persons, sin is any act or thought that does not measure up to what God expects of us. That means that all of us sin. (Show me a person who says he or she has never sinned, and I'll show you a liar.)

If you have been taught that to masturbate is bad, then you will feel it's wrong. However, most of the major Protestant churches in America have no official church statements on the subject. They don't seem too concerned about it. The same is true for some Catholic leaders. A priest once told me, "Our church considers it a sin, but not very much." His point was this: If one has fantasies about another person while masturbating, it might be a sin for two reasons. First, the person might be tempted to make that fantasy come true. Second, Jesus said, "Anyone who looks at a woman [or man?] lustfully has already committed adultery with her in his heart" (Matt. 5:27). That is, you may reduce the person to just a sex object.

However, it must be noted that other Catholic leaders—and some Protestant ones—take a different view. For example, the Vatican views masturbation as a serious sin. Sex is seen as a gift of God to be shared, but only in marriage. It has a twofold purpose in the marriage: for procreation, and as a means of mutual sharing of love—but only between spouses. Since masturbation centers the sex expression on the self, it is thought to be an abuse of the purpose of sex. Masturbation is not evil or bad in itself; it's just that it violates the principle that sex is to be shared, and only with one's spouse.

Still another view of masturbation is taken by some leaders of various religions. They argue that masturbation for pleasure is not wrong in itself unless someone is being hurt by it. They hold that God created human beings to be sexual persons for three reasons, not just one or two. Certainly sex is for the all-important role of procreation. We share that with all the rest of God's creatures. But two facts, they say, prove that God created human sexuality for two other reasons as well. First, it is for personal pleasure, in masturbation or in marriage, as long as one's mate is not robbed of joy. It is also a unique way for two married persons to join their total personalities into a joyful sharing of their love for each other.

One bit of evidence they cite is that human beings are the only species that is created so that we usually engage in sex in a face-to-face love embrace. Did God make a mistake in creating us that way? Or did God mean for us to use sex also as a way of sharing love?

The other bit of evidence is that, unique among all creatures, human females are the only ones who will permit, and even want, sex at times other than when they can get pregnant. Every other female rejects the male except when she is ready to conceive. Again, did God make a mistake? Or did God mean to make human sexuality something to share with joy?

Those who follow this line of reasoning hold that the Lord made no mistake. God planned it exactly that way—and it is good. Therefore they say that masturbation for pleasure is not wrong.

A further point. One important role our sex urge plays is to make us notice and make friends with those of the opposite sex. It nudges us in their direction. That is good. But if one masturbates too much, that urge may be decreased. The result? No nudging. As one girl put it in the film, *Sexuality and Communications*,[3] "You don't meet too many nice people that way."

All in all, it seems doubtful that masturbation is considered to be much of a sin by your religion. But check it out with your priest, minister, or rabbi. If your religion is against it, you will likely feel guilty if you do it.

80 Why do people masturbate? That's gross!

If that is the way you feel, then don't do it. It would be wrong for you.

81 People say that male masturbation is normal, but after trying it I did not enjoy it, so I stopped. It has been over two years and I still have no desire to do it again. I also had intercourse two times and I didn't enjoy that either. . . . Am I abnormal in some way because I do not masturbate?

No one is abnormal just because they don't do something that most other people do. However, it is not normal not to enjoy any sexual stimulation like masturbating or sexual intercourse. You will likely need a good physical exam and/ or some counseling sometime in the future. Meanwhile, just go about your business of being young and the best student you can be. While in high school, it's not smart to get too involved in sex anyway.

82 If premarital sex is not a good idea, but the couple has had a long courtship and mutual sex attraction, what do you recommend to prevent sexual intercourse?

That decision must be yours. You have a number of choices.

I do think you are very wise to reject premarital sex. There are just too many ways it can mess up your life now and in the future. It's best to wait.

You can, of course, abstain. You can use will-power—or "won't power." No one has to have sex. Many go without having sex for years or a lifetime without negative results. This has never caught on with the masses, but it's one option.

Another choice is to decide together how far down what I call the "road to arousal" of necking and petting that you (or you two) think you should go. Go no farther. Express your emotions up to a point, and then stop.

Or you can "sublimate" the sex urges. That is, you can firmly decide to do other things as substitutes for giving in to your sex drive. It could be sports, exercise, art, or some hobby—almost anything that holds your interest. This can distract your attention away from thoughts of sex.

Some people have used masturbation as an out, since it takes the edge off the desire and has no known ill effects. It makes more sense than to give in to the urge to have intercourse. But of course, it is not a choice for those who worry a lot about it, or who feel it's a sin.

If you really want to save intimate sex for marriage, you can do that. It will help if you steer clear of the kinds

81

of things that tempt you. You can avoid the R-rated or X-rated movies, books, or magazines that are likely to arouse your sex urges. Try to stay away from situations with your dates where having sex would be easy. Avoid being with the person in a house when parents or others are not around, for instance. Or parking in lonely spots for long periods of time. Or double-dating with couples that you think will have sex with each other in your presence. Exposing yourself to these kinds of situations is just asking for trouble.

It may also help to keep in mind what a woman once wrote to "Dear Abby": "You often receive letters from young girls asking: 'Should I or should I not go all the way before marriage?' I was given a beautiful reason why I should not, and I never forgot it. There were no heavy warnings or confusing explanations. It was simply this: 'Intimacy between man and woman is God's wedding gift to the new-lyweds, and [this] gift is not to be opened early.'"

PART 7

How Can I Know When It's Love?

83 Why do scientists such as yourself make love out to be so complex when in fact it should be one of the simplest things in life—a natural human instinct?

It is just such false ideas that lead to so many divorces. It suggests that when the right person for you comes along, you will "just know." Not so. You can't just trust your heart. If there is any instinct involved, it is the deep desire to mate and to breed. Lower animals do that, too. Then often the male cuts out and leaves the female to cope with rearing the cubs.

Most humans are more responsible than that—or at least we should be. We realize that rearing children is a most complex matter. We need to give them training in hundreds of ways if they are to grow up to be good citizens. Both fathers and mothers have a role to play in the process.

"Mating" is far more than choosing a convenient sex-mate. It is the matching of two unique persons in many, many aspects of their lives. You can't just pick a good mate by instinct. We need all the help we can get to succeed— from science and anywhere else we can get it.

84 Should you rely more on logic or feeling when making a choice?

Both are important. All logic and no feeling makes for a very dull marriage. But all feeling and no logic leads to tragic mistakes and mismatching of mates. I like to quote the old Greek wise men. They said, "Emotion must warm reason, but reason must rule emotion." Best to have a good balance of the two.

Science and research can give us a lot of aid. It can help us avoid the awful pitfalls of the past, and lead us to do a better job of mate choice in the future.

85 **I am very confused. One day I am just sure that my girlfriend is the one for me. The next day I have doubts. How can I sort it all out and come up with the right answer? My folks got a divorce and I sure don't want to go through that mess again.**

If you have all these doubts, it's wise to wait.

You do want to avoid a mistake at the altar. As of now, the odds that one's first marriage will succeed are no more than even. Some now put that at two out of three. One out of two first marriages now ends in divorce. Another three percent of married couples become separated. And eight to ten percent tough it out but are not at all happy. Unless you learn to beat those odds, there's only a flip of the coin, heads-or-tails chance that your marriage will work out. Those wedding bells are just as likely to ring out sad, not glad tidings.

What you are asking is how you can tell if you have now found a love that will last. From my own research I have found this to be the number one courtship question that youth and young adults want answered. Even older people want to know how to tell if they have real love.

86 **What is puppy love? Is a crush a kind of infatuation?**

Puppy love and a crush are the same thing. My term for it is *Primary Infatuation*. It involves putting some person on a pedestal. You idealize them. At times, you might almost worship them. It, for the most part, involves a younger person having such strong feelings toward a much older one. Like a student for a teacher. Or like a teenager and a rock star. In each case, the person is "out of reach" for the one who has the crush. To that extent, it is likely a harmless, passing thing.

We must contrast that with *Romantic Infatuation,* which is more likely to happen between two persons of similar age. It is far more dangerous, since the couple are more inclined to do something foolish about it, such as getting deeply into sex. Or marrying in haste in the heat of emotion. They will usually regret it, but then it is too late.

A love relation is indeed very complex. Some people mistake romance, falsely called "Romantic Love," for real love. It's not love at all. To call it love is a fraud, a falsehood. It only leads to confusion and delusion. That is why I call it "Romantic Infatuation" and not Romantic Love.

Such a romance will hold a marriage intact no more than three to five years, even with a red-hot sex life thrown in. In time, sex gets less and less exciting. It loses much of its ability to keep beckoning the two back together via the bed. Some of its former fervor fades.

Romance does soon fade in a marriage. How many couples can you name who, after 10 years of marriage, still have romantic dinners with soft music and candles every day? Or once a week? Or even once a month? And there's not much romance in washing dishes, cleaning floors, and taking out the garbage—even if a couple does them together.

No, a marriage based on romance just won't make it. Five years tops, and the tied knot will come loose.

On the other hand, many people think their strong sexual attraction for each other is a sure sign of love. Not so.

One can have strong sex attraction with or without romance, and with or without love.

Since my students were so confused about true love, I spent some 30 years in search of answers to the puzzle. The full results are set forth in my book, *Sex, Love, or Infatuation: How Can I Really Know?* There I describe "Fourteen Key Clues" by which one can distinguish true love from false love. It is probably the most complete summary of what scientists know on this subject now in print.

These clues seem to be helping many people "sort it all out." I do think that if you apply these 14 clues honestly and with due care, you will come up with a pretty clear answer to your question. It won't be possible in this book to fully explain all 14 clues. But let's now review some of the clues which will, and those which will not, be useful signs of love. Consider the following questions:

87 **Since I met this boy, I just haven't been the same. I daydream about him all the time. I can't study or do my work. I've even lost my appetite. My mom says I'm in love. Is she right?**

You've described a "false clue." You may be in love, or just infatuated. I've devised 14 Key Clues to help tell the difference.

True love will have symptoms that are quite different—often opposite—from the symptoms that describe infatuation. That is the case for each of the 14 clues. There will be clear contrast.

The three "false clues," on the other hand, are tricky. They can be present in *either* true or false love. If you have any of those three symptoms, it can just as easily indicate one as the other. You just can't trust them. Let's review these three false clues so you can be on your guard against them.

(1) You will get *funny feelings,* especially when you're near to, or thinking of the other person. These strange feelings occur whether you have romantic infatuation or real love. Your heart may flutter or pound. Your tummy may feel strange. Your knees may get weak. You may clam up or find it hard to talk to that person. Or, as you say, you may daydream a lot and not even want to eat. Don't be fooled. This does not mean it's love at all.

(2) *A gnawing need for nearness* is a second false sign. You long to be with each other all the time. You can scarcely stand it when you have to be apart, even for just a little while. You seem pulled together like a nail to a magnet. But don't send for Marryin' Sam. It may only be sex or romance again. It may not be love at all. It's another false clue.

(3) Finally, be it love or infatuation, you are likely to have a *powerful pull to passion.* You really turn each other on. The sex urge haunts you like a ghost. But don't be duped. The fact that your breath comes in short pants each time you touch each other is not a sign of true love. Sex attraction can be just as strong in a romantic infatuation as it is in the real thing. And in some cases, it may be sex and nothing more that turns you on.

In sum, you can have one or more of these symptoms—even all of them—and still not be in love. Don't be fooled. You need the other 14 clues to tell you whether it is real love. The findings of science can help you make a sound decision.

While we're on the subject of showing affection, is it OK to do it in public? Have you known couples who lean against each other very suggestively right out in front of God and everybody? Or French kiss—I call it a tongue-in-cheek kiss—and moan like a porcupine in pain? Well, get a load of this! Psychologists have found a strong tie between people who express a lot of affection in public and the low scores they make on emotional maturity tests! So the next time you see a couple making a public display you can say to them: "I know something about you!!" They may get the point and clean up their act.

And it makes sense. Mature people who really love and respect each other don't wear their passion on their sleeves. Passion is something special to be done only in private, not displayed in public.

88 How can I know when I've found the right person to marry?

You can tell a true love from a false one by asking yourself those 14 key questions. You should reply to each of them truthfully and with careful thought. If you do that, in most cases you will quickly see whether it's love. Here are the questions:

CLUE 1. What is your main interest in the other person? What attracts you most?

CLUE 2. How many things about the person attract you?

CLUE 3. How did the romance start?

CLUE 4. How consistent is your level of interest?

CLUE 5. What effect does the romance have on your personality?

CLUE 6. How did it end?

CLUE 7. How do you two view each other?

CLUE 8. How do others view you two? What's the attitude of friends and families?

CLUE 9. What does distance (long separation) do to the relationship?

CLUE 10. How do quarrels affect the romance?

CLUE 11. How do you feel about and refer to your relationship?

CLUE 12. What's your ego response to the other?

CLUE 13. What's your overall attitude toward the other?

CLUE 14. What is the effect of jealousy?

Now we will look more closely at a few of the clues just to show you how they work.

CLUE 1: What is *the main thing that attracts me* to him or her? If it's that person's *physical equipment,* then it points to infatuation. You mainly like the face or figure, the smile, the way he or she walks or talks.

In real love, the physical things are not the main concern. It's not the mask of the face, but what's behind that mask that counts. The shape of the body is far less important to you than what's housed *in* the body. You like the person's mind, emotions, attitudes, and goals. In short, your main attraction is to the *total personality,* not just one part of it. It's the kind of person you respect, care a lot about, and like to be around. As young people put it these days, he or she is a beautiful person. So his ears are too big. They stick out like a scared baby elephant. Or she's as flat-chested as your Uncle Charlie. So what? Your main interest should not be looks.

Men tend to trip up on this score more than women. When I was a young man, our high school held a "for men only" assembly. We were all ears, thinking we would hear something really juicy. We didn't. But one thing the guy said stuck with me all these years. "Fellows," he said, "don't make the mistake that a lot of guys do. A lot of guys pass up a beautiful woman to marry a pretty girl." Sad to say, a lot of men are still doing just that.

89 **Do you think that people must always have something in common with each other to make a good relationship?**

Yes, by all means. And the more the better. That leads us neatly into . . .

CLUE 2: How many things attract you to that person? If it's infatuation, the answer will be *few* things. This clue may sound simpler than it is. False or romantic "love" (infatuation) can trip you up. Why? Because those few things you *do* like about the person may be felt very strongly. That may fool you into thinking you have more things in common than you really do. Be on your guard. Count with caution.

If it's real love, *many or most* of the things about the person will attract you. What about the way he or she thinks? Reactions to failure and success? Attitudes toward people? How about goals in life? Plans for the future? Likes and dislikes? The more of these hundreds of things about the person's whole self that you like and admire and respect, the greater the chance that your love is real. And by the way, have you ever had doubts that you are important? If so, just think about this.

Of the billions of people on this earth, you are unique. There has never ever been even one other person just like you! You are one of a kind, hence of very special worth. What a wonderful thought that is! So don't ever let anyone try to tell you you're not important. You are uniquely important.

If you take that to heart, it will put real meaning and purpose in your life. When God made you, God threw the mold away. There won't be many suicides if people take that seriously.

90 Is there such a thing as love at first sight?

Romantic infatuation at first sight, yes. Love? No way.

CLUE 3: How did the romance start? Romance and sex attraction can strike like a bolt out of the blue. And it can disappear just as fast. You know the old story. Rogers and

Hammerstein put it into words and music in *South Pacific:* "Some enchanted evening" . . . two eyes meet across a crowded room—and they know. That's pure poppycock. THEY DON'T KNOW ANYTHING. At least not about love.

Real love can only start slowly. Each person is very complex, with many different traits and qualities. Some of these are obvious but many are not. So you can't possibly know enough about someone in a few moments, a few days, or even a few weeks to be sure you want to spend the rest of your life together. That decision takes time—lots of time—two years or more.

CLUE 6: *How did your relationship end?* Answer: the same way it started. *False loves stop fast* and *true loves stop slowly.* This is true in two different ways. First, if you break up, you are more likely to get over an infatuation in a short while. Only a few surface things attracted you, so there's not all that much to get over. But with love, many things attracted you. Your personalities came to be intertwined in a lot of ways. It may take years to get over such a deep relationship. Indeed, in some ways you may never be the same again.

A second thing to watch for is how long the relationship lasts while it is going on. In most cases, false loves don't last long. There aren't many things the couples have in common. There isn't much that they like to talk about or do together. Therefore, they lose interest quite quickly. By and large, infatuations won't last more than a few weeks or months. There is one exception. I'll explain that in a moment.

Real loves last many months and years, often for one's whole life. Whole blocks of the two personalities are in harmony. Each has become a very real part of the other. So if a relationship has lasted a long time, that is usually a good sign of love. And again, the longer you have a good relationship before marriage, the better the chance your marriage will be for keeps. This is called passing the "test of time."

There is just one catch, though. You can flunk that all-important test of time. How? By getting involved deeply in sex too soon. If in your courtship you get into a sexual relation that is fully satisfying to both of you, the test of time just won't work for you. You have cheated on the test.

You see, the sex urge is very deep and urgent in each of us. A couple with a good sexual relation but with very little else may well be held together for as much as three to five years. It is the satisfying sex, not the more solid cement of a good overall relationship, that keeps you coming back to each other. So you can be fooled. You may think that since your relationship has lasted a couple of years, it has passed the test of time. It hasn't. It may have been little more than sex that kept you together.

This is perhaps the strongest reason of all why it is unwise for a couple to go all the way with sex before they marry. That sex can lead them into a tragic marriage, likely to fail in a year or two. A couple thus robs themselves of the very best natural protection they have against getting into a bad marriage.

91 **My guy and I get along just fine, but our parents don't approve of our relationship. Does that really matter?**

It matters a lot. In fact, that is one of the Key Clues to tell you if it's love.

CLUE 8: What's the attitude of friends and family? Research reported as recently as 1992 affirms that parents still have a strong role in influencing romantic relations in the United States today. Negative reactions by friends and families to a couple tend to deteriorate the relationship. In turn, good support leads to a higher quality of it. Approval is important both in courtship and in marriage.

Perceived support from one's own family and friends has a large influence on the satisfaction, love, and commitment of the person.

And doesn't that make sense? After all, who loves and cares more about you and your future than your close friends and your family? If they see you getting into a situation that they think will bring you heartache and tragedy, of course they will turn thumbs down. But if they think it will lead to happy times for you down the line, they'll be all for it.

It's best to bend your ears to what your loved ones think. They have an advantage. They don't have stars in their eyes.

92 **What are the odds of our breaking up when my boyfriend goes away to college?**

The answer suggests another Key Clue.

CLUE 9: What does distance (long separation) do to the relationship? If you have real love for your friend—many things you like and admire and respect—you have nothing to worry about. That person actually will have become a part of your very being. When he or she is not there, you are not all there. A part of you is away. So you both will long to be united again with that other part of yourselves. You won't like to be apart, but your love is likely to survive.

But if your relation was surface—physical attraction to what you can see, hear, smell, taste, or touch about the other—it likely will die. Out of sight, out of mind. Other physical equipment that is more available at the moment will lead you to forget your former flame. It was probably tough to take at the time, but such a breakup is a good thing in the long run.

The next two clues go together. They are similar, but for the sake of clarity and the greater emphasis they deserve, we will treat them as if they were separate.

CLUE 12: Are you selfish or selfless with regard to the other person? This is an acid test. And it is a rough one. It's hard to be honest enough to admit that we are selfish, so we tend to deny it.

But honest we must be if we are to learn the truth. If you are infatuated, *your ego response is largely selfish and possessive*. Your big question about the relationship is: "What am I going to get out of this?" You're looking out for number one. You are self-serving. You may even use the other person for your own gain. She dates him because he has a good set of wheels. He dates her to get sex thrills or peer praise. Each has an ego big enough to choke a mule. And that chokes off love as well.

When you really love another, you want all the same good things for that person that you want for yourself. *Your ego response is largely selfless*. Your own pleasure and happiness are in great part tied in with that of your beloved. To paraphrase the late President John F. Kennedy, you "ask not what your beloved can do for you, but what you can do for your beloved."

CLUE 13: What is your overall attitude? This clue is similar to the previous one. For the infatuated person, the basic attitude is one of *taking from the relationship*. Your interest is measured in terms of gain and loss. You take all you can get. You give little thought to what harm it may do to the other. You may not admit it, even to yourself, but it's true. You like the person not for what she or he *is,* but for what that person can do for *you.*

To love, on the other hand, is to really care about the other. Your overall attitude is that of giving, not taking. You will look for ways you can make the other happy and fulfilled. You don't just give the other good treatment and gifts in order to get something back. You give whether or not you get in return. It gives you joy just to see your beloved's joy. If you really love, your giving is its own reward.

There's a warning here for girls. We scientists have long known that young women at this age take their relationships more seriously than do the men. If a girl goes with a guy very long, she likely thinks a lot of him. She may even think she loves him.

So if some night in a lonely spot he whispers in her shell-pink ear: "Honey, if you love me you'll let me," you might be tempted to give him sex. After all, you love him and it's quite obvious what he has in mind.

But before you get sucked in by that old line, girls, ask yourself a few questions. Who will get the blame if someone finds out? Who will risk getting pregnant? Who runs the greatest risk of getting STDs and AIDS? Clearly you are the one who will get hurt the most.

So may I suggest, girls, if he whispers: "If you love me you'll let me," why not whisper back: "Honey, if you really love me. If you really care about me and my future, you won't ask me to." And you know what? He won't, either. If he really loves you, he will not want to expose you to all those risks. Not if he really loves you.

A *Sum-up Clue:* Each of these 14 Key Clues is important. Each will tell you something special about your relationship that you really need to know. But no one or two, or even four or five, taken by themselves out of the list, is enough to give you the accurate answer you need. So answer each of the questions as honestly and sensibly as you can.

But if I had to come up with just one clue as a test of true love, it would be this one from *Sex, Love or Infatuation.* It cuts to the core. No one clue by itself is enough, but this one comes close:

> *If you love someone so much that you want that person to be happy, even if you are not the one to make him or her happy, then you really love that person.* That is, if you love someone so much that you want that person to be happy, even if you can't be the one who *shares* that happiness, then your love is indeed real.

There you have it. Your wish to do what is best for your beloved is even more important to you than that gnawing need to be the one to share love with him or her. That test will quickly separate those who have real love from those who do not.

Sorting out love is a tough process. If it's a problem for you, be sure to consult the more complete discussion of it in *Sex, Love, or Infatuation*. There you will find the symptoms for love and infatuation listed in a check-chart.

How can you use the clues? A fairly valid measure of your relationship can be obtained just by counting up your answers. Which of them fall into the infatuation column, and which belong in the love column?

But not all of your answers will in every case be either/or. Instead some may be both/and. For example, there are *degrees* of jealousy. Some relationships start very fast, some only fairly fast. So we have devised an easy way to score your relationship more accurately. Simply score yourself on each of the clues (except the one, "How does it stop?") on a scale of zero to ten:

Your Score	What It Means	Suggested Action
0–50	Infatuation	Cool it; make no promises, no commitments.
50–90	Toss-up	Some hope; shows promise, but give it more time.
90–130	Real love	Consider marriage—with due care.[1]

How best to use this chart to assess your own situation is fully explained in the 1990 edition of *Sex, Love, or Infatuation: How Can I Really Know?*

93 Can one person be in love and the other only infatuated?

Yes, and it happens a lot. But unless the infatuated person develops love, it won't work. Watch closely to see

if that is in fact happening as determined by using the
Key Clues.

94 Can infatuation turn into love?

Yes. Give it time and keep checking the clues to see
which direction it seems to be going.

95 Is it possible to be in love more than once?

Of course. If that were not true, a lot of people would
have to spend most of their life alone. No two loves are
exactly alike, but you really can love several times in your
lifetime.

96 Can one just be in love with love?

Oh yes. You can just feel the need for romance. But that
is not really love in the sense I'm talking about. Best to
cool it.

97 Is it possible to be in love with more than one
person at the same time?

It is quite possible and happens quite often, according
to the research. You can also be infatuated with two people
at the same time. And you can be in love with one and
infatuated with another at the same time. You can really
mix it up—and be really mixed up in the process.

98 How do you get over an infatuation? And how
do you get over a lost love?

The answer to both questions is about the same. In time,
your heart will heal. I know; that is very hard to accept
while the hurt is so deep. But believe me. It is true.

It will take much longer to recover if it was love. In some ways you may never quite bury the hurt. But in time, it will grow less and less. You can just count on that.

The main thing to remember is not to do something foolish like thinking about seclusion or even suicide. That would not be wise at all. Just turn your attention to other things. Remove all reminders of that person. Take that picture out of your billfold. Maybe burn it. Then bury yourself in other interests—your studies, your other friends, your family, your hobbies. Soon you will begin to feel better, and in time you will wonder why it gave you such a bad time to lose the relationship.

99 Can you fall out of true love?

That can happen. No matter how careful you are to pick the right mate, marriage does involve some risk. The person you are now married to may not be the same kind of person you married. For instance, you may have married a moderate drinker. Now you are living with an alcoholic. Or a physical abuser. Or a compulsive gambler. Or a drug addict. Or one who cheats on you. You may not be able to love that changed person in the same way you did before.

Some may still love in spite of the changes. For others, these new behaviors may kill the love they once had for their mate.

But for many—we hope most—of us marrieds, we are glad for the choice we made.

If you use them with caution, these 14 Key Clues will serve you well. In most cases the type of relationship you have will become quite clear.

PART 8

Teen Sex: Time to Sound the Alarm

How sad that we have reached a point in the United States where the parent of a student could ask the following question.

100 Why do people think there's something wrong with a male or female who does not want to get sexually involved?

Not too long ago this question would not have been asked. That it can be asked now is a reflection of much of the current fuzzy thinking about sex. In my view, it is a dangerous direction. Many people do not yet realize that the ones who abstain are the smart ones.

There is only one thing "wrong" with those who don't get involved in sex. It is that they dare to have moral and sensible values in the face of great pressures. Those who get into sex are the foolish ones, as we shall soon see.

101 Are young people all that much more into sex before marriage now than they have been before?

The following chart, based on recent research, gives us the answer.

FIGURE 1.

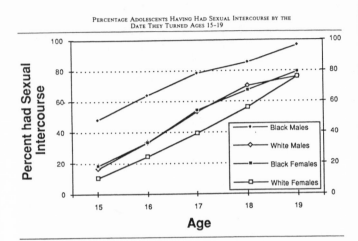

PERCENTAGE ADOLESCENTS HAVING HAD SEXUAL INTERCOURSE BY THE DATE THEY TURNED AGES 15–19

Source: Brent C. Miller, from data in Moore, Snyder, and Daly, 1992. Used by permission.[1]

Note that the increase in numbers of sexually active teenagers has risen in almost straight lines from age 15. About half the girls were into sex by age 18, but this percentage rose to three-fourths by age 19. From this trend, it is clear why the rates of teen pregnancy and STDs are rising apace.

When they had their first sex, the girl's partner was about three years older than she.[2] That's why I hold that at high school age or younger, it is not wise to date one-to-one alone with anyone more than a year or two older or younger than oneself. It would seem that many of the older boys are just waiting to pounce on the younger girls.

And this may shock you. One school principal told me that the upperclass boys spoke of the freshman girls as—would you believe? Fresh meat! Freshman girls, take note.

For most white females, their first sex "just happened" with someone they were dating or going steady with. And for a rather large number, first sex was forced: 6.3 percent of females, .04 percent of males.[3]

Past sexual abuse is quite high for three groups of girls:

1. Girls in foster care or on welfare

2. Girls with teenage mothers

3. Girls whose parents drank or used drugs[4]

After their first sex, women tend to have multiple partners. By 16 months after first intercourse, at least half of those age 15–17 had more than one partner. By 19 months, three-fourths had. By two-and-one-half years after their first sex, 90 percent had had two or more partners.[5] Postponing the time of first intercourse would be a big step in decreasing the incidence of multiple partners.

Youth get into sex at younger and younger ages, but marry later and later. And they are at real risk of getting STDs, AIDS, or becoming pregnant. In one study, of all the women who had had sex in the last three months, fully 79 percent were at such risk.[6] The effect of these kinds of behaviors on the rise in the number of abortions is also clear.

Small wonder that as teen sex becomes more frequent, so does the concern of society. That is encouraging. More and more parents, pastors, school teachers and staff, and youth workers are deeply concerned about these problems. The teen sex statistics do not bode well for the future of the family and of our children. Even scientists and medical experts seem to be catching on, as well as a few members of Congress.

A congressional panel led by Rep. Patricia Schroeder, D-Col., has expressed alarm at the spread of AIDS among our adolescents. The panel even condemned the federal government's response to the crisis as "a national disgrace."

Their panel report came out in April, 1992. In it they noted that "the number of teens who have AIDS increased by more than 70 percent in the preceding two years." And that doesn't even take into account the number of teens with the HIV virus who have not yet developed AIDS.

This is indeed cause for alarm. AIDS is now the sixth leading cause of death among youth ages 15–19.[7] Isn't it time we wake up to the impact of this situation and begin to educate our young to the wisdom of not doing it? And to pass the word that to be a virgin should be a source of high praise, not shame? And that they should wear the badge of virginity with great pride?

A program called "True Love Waits" urges youth to sign a pledge to postpone sex until marriage. Readers may wish to contact them.*

102 It seems the media and research always stress the teens who are creating the problem. Why do we hear nothing about the many teens who are not?

You are so right. We are guilty. We learn that over 10 percent of the girls have had sex before they reach age 15. That is too many. But that means that almost 90 percent have *not* done so. If 50 percent have lost their virginity by their 17th year, the other 50 percent have not.

One researcher admits that our stress tends to be too negative. Studies "virtually ignore the still substantial fraction of teens who do not engage in sexual intercourse."[8]

*Send to: BSSB, 127-9th Avenue North, Nashville, TN, 37234, or call toll free 1-800-458-2772. Tell them Ray Short sent you!

I guess our position has been if it isn't broke, don't fix it. So we put our stress on the part that does need fixing and neglect to praise the fine teens who resist the urge to get active. They deserve a hearty round of applause.

We do see some good signs on the horizon. True, society has been more accepting of premarital sex, mainly among the younger set. But from 1974 to 1991, the views of young adults aged 18-35 have changed a great deal. Whereas in 1974, 12 percent thought premarital sex and adultery were always wrong, 18 percent now think so.[9] That's an increase of 50 percent.

The percentage is still too low, but at least it is moving in the right direction. As these young adults marry and have teens of their own, they seem to get a bit less permissive in their views. Until more do so, however, we will still have a big problem. Another good sign. Having sex with multiple partners is again being thought immoral. In one study, 64 percent of the women thought it was immoral if women did it, 52 percent if men did it. Among the men, over half thought it immoral if women had multiple partners, but less than a third thought so if men did.[10] The double standard is still alive and well, even among the women. As the old song puts it: "When will they ever learn?"

103 Why are so many adolescents having sexual intercourse, and at such young ages now?

As one might expect, the reasons for starting to have sex early is different for females than for males. Females are more influenced by the opinions and values of persons they feel close to. Males respond more to the nudges from their hormones.

Teens differ in life goals. Those who are sexually active place a higher value on personal independence. In turn, they place lower value on grades in school. They are more tolerant of deviant behavior and are less religious.

Here are more reasons why youth get into sex, and so early.

1. The younger they are when they reach puberty, the younger they will start to have sex. Their ability to have sex outruns their emotional ability to control it.

2. They cannot foresee the long term effects of their sex acts. About 83 percent of experienced males later realize that they got into sex too young. They wish they had not started sex so soon.[11]

3. Teens tend to be risk-takers. They think they can take chances and not have to pay the price. When they find they are not immune, it is too late.

4. There is less fear of pregnancy. Birth control is now more effective and easy to get.

5. Many see abortion as an out if they do take chances and get caught.

6. More young people today believe sex before marriage is not as bad as their parents think. They assume that society also accepts it, though as a whole it does not.

7. Peer pressure leads many to think that "everyone's doing it." In some groups that may be true, but for the most part it is not. Lots of youth are still virgins and plan to stay that way. Remember: half of the girls at age 17 are virgins.

8. The Vietnam War led many youth to doubt not only patriotic values ("my country, right or wrong but nonetheless, my country") but also moral and religious

norms. They said, "If it feels good, then do it." If pre-marital sex is wrong, youth now demand to know why. And they deserve straight answers.

9. It's easier now to be alone. In most colleges, there are co-ed dorms with no limit to hours spent together in rooms. For those who are younger, there are the back seats of cars—or right in a parent's home. If both mom and dad work, there's often a gap of a couple of hours between the time school is out and the folks get home. A lot can happen in two hours—or even in eight minutes!

10. The women's movement is a factor. Some women see their equality as freedom to have sex on an equal basis with men. What they fail to remember is that the men don't get pregnant, women do. And women are also more likely to get STDs in coitus.

11. There is now less fear of getting a bad name from a neighborhood gossip. As more people move to large cities, the social pressure to behave is less. The girl in Podunk Corners must heed a meddlesome gossip or pay a price. The city girl will likely just tell "the old snoop" to go fly a kite—or worse.

12. Many parents and churches have failed to give moral guidance in matters of sex.

13. More explicit sex on TV, in the movies, in rap songs, and in novels shape teen views of sex.

14. We all face an uncertain future. As a result, many opt for the quick thrills of sex. Let's explore this one a bit more, since it's often overlooked.

Dr. George Wald, Nobel Prize winner in biology at Harvard, has called this, "the generation in search of a future."

Youth today have never known what it is to feel secure. Every moment of their lives they have been under the constant, day-after-day threat of being wiped out at any time by a nuclear bomb.

Dr. Wald was asked if he, as a biologist, thought our space explorers would ever find intelligent life on other planets. His reply came as quite a shock. "My main concern is whether when our spacemen come back to earth they will find intelligent life here." A sobering thought indeed. It is no wonder that many of our young people opt for the quick thrills in life rather than the long-term values.

When the future is in doubt, many rush into rash decisions. When we are at war, couples rush into sex or even marriage. They fear that tomorrow will not come for them.

In World War II some girls gave sex to men in the service. Their excuse was, "They're risking their lives for me, so I'll give them the joy of sex." I once hitchhiked from Oregon to a seminar in Eastern Canada. A soldier picked me up to help him drive. He then picked up two young women, one of them married to a sailor serving in Europe. While I drove, she had sex with that stranger right there in the backseat of his car. She excused it as her patriotic duty! I wonder how patriotic her sailor husband would have thought she was.

I recently linked the nuclear threat to teen sex at a Senate subcommittee hearing. A wire service picked up the quote, "If I don't get sex now, I may never get to know what it feels like." A woman sent me a note that read in part:

"I have just read your article: 'Bomb fear a factor in teen sex?' in the Miami *Herald*. . . . I'm a survivor of the (Nazi) Holocaust. . . . The point that you have brought up: 'If I don't get sex now, I'll never know what it feels like' . . . was a very essential part of life during the Holocaust."

Few of us would condone such behavior, but it does happen. If we are to curb foolish and irresponsible teen sex, we must put a stop to this insane nuclear arms race which is still with us. And there is danger that such bombs will fall into hostile hands like a terrorist or a ruthless dictator.

We have to provide enough responsible world law with justice so that nations have to settle their disputes through courts of law, just like everybody else. War with such weapons is utter nonsense. We need to settle our differences by legal, not lethal methods. I think it's time we all join with the Campaign for U.N. Reform and the World Federalist Association in their efforts to have nations settle disputes peaceably through the force of law, not the law of force. It's a most worthy cause for any of us who want to see our children and grandchildren, as well as ourselves, have a secure future.[12]

104 Is there any way to tell which adolescents are more—or less—likely to get into sex at an early age?

The findings of science can help us. Here are some things that may influence a young person's behavior.[13]

Positive Influences

1. Have biological father in home
2. See sex acts and marriage as connected
3. Have parents with stable marriage
4. Received sex education from parents
5. Have well-educated, affluent parents with higher life goals

Negative Influences

Have single parent or stepfather

See sex and marriage as separate

Have single parent who is dating or cohabiting

Received no sex education in the home

Have poor parents with low education and lower life goals

6. Attend all-white schools	Attend racially mixed schools
7. Don't smoke, drink, do drugs	Do smoke, drink, do drugs
8. Is a white or Chicano male	Is a Black or Latino male
9. Have high occupational desire	Have low occupational desire
10. Have high self-esteem when younger	Have high self-esteem when older
11. Shows strong self-control	Yields to other/peer control
12. Is active in religious matters	Shows little interest in religion

A few important comments. *A youth's future or behavior is not determined* by having one or more of these factors. It does mean that those who have negative elements are more at risk for having sex at an earlier age. With proper motivation a young person can overcome some or even all of these handicaps.

Number 10 is of special interest. At an early age, high self-esteem tends to shield a youth from early sex. But at an older age, high self-esteem is associated with greater chances of getting into sex. Higher self-esteem tends to lead them to be more bold in initiating sexual contacts.

105 What can we do to turn this adolescent sex epidemic around?

Dr. Brent C. Miller has come up with a clever way of outlining five choices we can pursue to stem the tide of too-soon sex.[14] These could also be used by any youth to make his or her own personal choice. Let's explore these options.

1. *Just say KNOW.* Get the facts about the risks and consequences of early sex. I've found that a strong stress on research facts, mixed with lots of humor and lively action, can turn many young students in the direction of not having sex. It works, at least for a while.

2. *Just say NO.* Take the pledge. Resolve not to have sex before commitment and marriage. Keeping the pledge may not be easy, but it can be done.

3. *Just say NOT YET.* Decide to wait for sex until you are willing and able to accept full responsibility for your actions.

4. *Just say NOT WITHOUT PROTECTION.* If you decide to do it in spite of the negative risks, then use the best available ways to avoid an unwanted pregnancy. As I like to put it: If you're going to do it, then for heaven's sake use your head as well as your tail!

5. *Just say I HAVE OTHER THINGS TO DO.* You can choose other more fruitful and less risky ways to spend your time now. You wait until you get a clearer vision of what you would like to do—and become—in the future. You don't wish to spoil that, so you refrain from any kind of behavior that might rob you of that future.

It's your choice. No one else can make it for you. But if you're smart and cool, you will think it through with great care and make the choice that seems to make the most sense. There are some signs of teen restraint of sex activity. True, 60 percent of teen males aged 15–19 say they've had sex. But how often? The mean number of partners in the past year was less than two. Frequency of intercourse was about once in every two weeks. On average they spent six months out of the last year with no partner at all. Only 21 percent had more than one partner in any month in the last year.[15]

PART 9

Premarital Sex: Look Before You Leap—into Bed

106 What is the difference between having sex and making love?

I'm glad you asked. There is a vast difference. Having sex may have nothing whatever to do with love. Two people—such as a call girl and her trick—can have sex without there being the slightest bit of love. They may be complete strangers. It can be a purely animal function with no affection at all. And that can happen with a teen couple in lover's lane as well.

No, it is impossible to "make" love. That's a false and dangerous concept. What you can do, though, is to share love through sex. But the love has to be there in the first place. Once two persons who love each other are married, every act of sex should be just that—a sharing of love with each other. To say you "make love" just cheapens what should be a beautiful experience for you both.

107 Please explain the "Road to Arousal." How far is *too* far?

The Road to Arousal describes the kind of behavior that leads to more and more sexual arousal. Early stages, like holding hands, won't likely arouse you very much. Heavy petting, on the other hand, likely will. Usually if you go much beyond serious kissing, you'll be breathing harder than if you'd just run a couple of blocks.

So you can be alerted to the facts, let's describe for you the stages that will probably arouse you more and more. The chart and discussion of it are taken from my book, *Sex, Love, or Infatuation.*[1]

The Road to Arousal

				Necking	Light petting			Heavy petting				
FULL REPRESSION	Holding hands	Hugging	Casual kissing	Serious kissing	French kissing (?)	Breasts covered.	Breasts bared	Genitals covered	Genitals bared	Oral sex (?)	Genital to genital	**SEXUAL INTERCOURSE**

Two of the stages are hard to place on the chart. French or deep kissing (what I call tongue-in-cheek kissing!) is by strict definition a last stage of necking. But its arousing effect on some may be so intense it could be classed as petting. (In the media such a kiss is followed by a trip to the bed. I hope you don't buy that nonsense.) Then again it may turn some people off completely. (Good grief—all those germs!) In like manner oral sex—mouth to genital—will likely have a negative effect on many people, especially women. (Yuck! I don't want my mouth *there!*) It is largely a male invention anyway.

So how far should you go down the Road to Arousal? And once you've set a limit on how far to go, how can you hold the line? You must find the right answers for yourself, but here are five general principles that may help you decide what is best for you.

PRINCIPLE 1. *Avoid the two extremes.* It is hazardous to go all the way before marriage. The long-term risks hardly seem worth the sensual thrills of the moment.

But it is equally dangerous to take the opposite extreme and fully repress the sex urge. If you try to keep the lid on it by refusing to admit it's there, you're failing to deal with it wisely. A repressed desire does not die. It just gets pushed out of the conscious mind and into the inner mind. There it smolders and festers, waiting its chance to be expressed in some other form. If you don't deal with it directly and consciously, it lurks in the shadows. It gets distorted and dangerous. Note this example from the past.

Jane was utterly ignorant about sex when she married John. In fact, when John kissed her once on a date she thought he had made her pregnant! (Hard to believe that she could think that, but she did!) During more than 25 years of marriage she saw sex as repulsive and dirty. She resisted all of John's normal advances. Several times she even tried to get doctors to prescribe that she should never have sex again.

Finally, as she approached menopause, I gave her a book aimed mainly at helping the inhibited wife. Later, as she returned it, tears streamed down her cheeks. "Oh, if only I'd read this book 30 years ago," she sobbed. "It would have saved me a lifetime of hell!" She had so repressed her sexuality that she and her husband were robbed of the normal joys of sharing their married love through sex.

In extreme cases, the sex urge may be denied (suppressed) so fully that it is in great measure destroyed. One law of biology is: Use it or lose it. Fish that live in caves with no light lose their sight. An arm that's never used will atrophy. A person confined to bed for many months must learn to walk all over again.

112

So it is with the sex urge. It is a fine and precious gift when used in the right way, but it can be a source of tragedy when it is not. It would seem wise for young people to give the sex urge enough expression to keep it warm and alive for marriage, while avoiding the dangers of its misuse.

It is hard to say which extreme holds the harsher hazards—total expression or total repression or suppression of the sex urge. Both can ruin lives. That's why the first principle is to *avoid both extremes.*

PRINCIPLE 2. *Don't light more fires than you put out.* If your goal is avoiding the two extremes, the trick is to give the sex drive a healthy expression without going too far. But how far is far enough?

The answer to that question may depend on your age and maturity. Or your level of willpower. Or your ability to keep control of yourself. Or your situation at a given time. Can you say no to yourself and others—and mean it?

Deciding how far to go will also depend on how well you know and like the other person. How long have you been seeing a lot of each other? How much can you trust the other person—and yourself? Are you willing to accept full responsibility for everything you do?

No one rule of thumb will apply in every case to every person. We are all different. Some may find that they must stop at necking. Others may find they can go farther with no real problems. You must determine for yourself how far down the Road to Arousal you can safely go.

But don't arouse more passion than you satisfy. If you do, you'll end up restless and frustrated and full of gnawing desire. If you're more disturbed and unhappy than you were to begin with, just what have you gained? Besides, you're probably skating on thin ice. Next time you may not be able to stop.

PRINCIPLE 3. *Avoid all chance of pregnancy.* This may strike you as strange. If you're not going to have intercourse, why worry about pregnancy?

As we have seen, a virgin can conceive. It doesn't happen often, but it is possible. Some doctors report that they come upon three or four cases every year.

Remember, sperm can wriggle their way up in the vagina, in through the cervix and uterus, into the fallopian tubes, and wham! Another virgin has conceived.

Hence, to avoid all chance of pregnancy, you must at the very least set your limit short of genital-to-genital petting. If you do pet until the male reaches climax, you must take care that none of the ejaculate is introduced to the vulva or vagina.

108 **What if a young woman does get pregnant outside of marriage?**

There's no really good answer. But let's consider her options.

If the father is mature and responsible and if they love each other, they can get married. They will have dozens of problems, but it may work out. But what if they have little or no foundation of love? Forced marriages are very high risk. Marriage might create worse problems for all concerned—the innocent baby included. A shotgun wedding can shoot down a couple's chances for a happy life and bring misery to the child.

Abortion may be *an out* for some, but it may *be out* for others. It's out for those who believe that a new human being exists from the moment of conception. To them, it really would be murder—and that's a heavy load of guilt to carry. Moreover, unless it is done under proper conditions, abortion can be highly dangerous, even fatal.

Or she may have the baby outside of marriage, but then she has another difficult choice to make. If she gives the baby up for adoption, in some states she may never again see her child, never know who has it, never know if it's alive or dead. Adoption may be best for her baby, but some women report that they continue to feel deep grief for years.

Each time they see a child the right age, they wonder: Could that one be mine?

The other choice is to keep her baby herself. Studies show that those who go this route score lower on maturity tests than those who choose adoption. That is partly because it's often done for selfish reasons. And it can be a rough road. There is still a stigma placed on both the unwed mother and her child, especially in rural and small-town America. The woman's chances to marry are fewer. She often ends up on welfare—at taxpayers' expense. Or her parents may have to help with the child's care and training. In all, the girl's dream of keeping her child may turn out to be a tragic nightmare. No woman ought to have to face an unwanted pregnancy. But if a couple is risking pregnancy, they'd better figure out what they will do when it occurs.

So where should sex play be halted before marriage? Some point short of where the girl has even the slightest chance of conceiving a child. Fun is fine as long as it doesn't spoil something better.

In view of all this, a lot of young people are concluding that sex before marriage just doesn't make good sense. It is *not* a disgrace to be a virgin. In fact, being a virgin is being smart.

PRINCIPLE 4. *Set your own limit—and stick to it.* Since it is your body, you have the right and the duty to decide what you do with it. It's a big decision. The stakes are high. Since you have only one body and one life to live, you'll want to claim the very most that life can offer.

So when you decide what your limit will be, you'll want it to be a sound, sober choice. You'll want to think it through beforehand and not wait until you're breathing hard in a red-hot petting session. You'll want your mind to rule your emotions, not the other way around. Follow your head, not your passion. It's best to call a firm halt to the process before there's even the slightest risk that you might lose your head—and with it your virtue.

And watch out for that old rattlesnake—*peer pressure*. Never mind what the couple in the back seat is doing. They may do that and not get pregnant or get an STD. You may do it in the front seat and get *both!*

Let's Shape Up, Guys

Some males think the female should be the one who puts the brakes on sex. But just because you're a guy, you are not excused. You need to be responsible and set limits on your own sexual behavior. You have the duty to act wisely just as much as the female has. If you want the woman you marry to be a virgin, you have no right to be other than a virgin for her.

The double standard is as old-fashioned as the Model T Ford. Why should it always be the woman who has to say "No!"? Why shouldn't we fellows take as much responsibility for our sperm as we expect her to take in protecting her ovum? In fact, it may soon become a legal duty.

A law in Wisconsin will no doubt spread to other states, because it is only fair. That law holds the male (and/or his parents) fully liable for half the costs of a pregnancy. If she has the baby and keeps it, *fathers are liable for half the costs of rearing that baby to age 18!* That could cost tens of thousands of bucks.

PRINCIPLE 5. *Couples who care, should share.* I'm a great believer in being honest in relationships. If you and another person come to care a great deal for each other, I think you should talk frankly about just how far you will go in sharing sexual affection. If you care enough about each other to want to go beyond casual kissing, then you know each other well enough to be frank about your feelings.

So before things go very far, talk it all over calmly in a serious, honest atmosphere. Let each other know how you feel. Decide together just where your limit is going to be.

116

Then both of you should take the moral duty to—as the cheerleaders say—"Hold that line! Hold that line!" If one of you threatens to lose control, then the other must call a halt.

But what if the male is not man enough to take his share of the burden? Then, alas, she must carry it all alone—fair or not. After all, she's the one who might take home a package her parents didn't order from WalMart.

109 Is sexual foreplay without sex as serious as sex itself?

Foreplay is touching each other in sexually sensitive parts of the body to bring pleasure and sexual excitement. It may be to prepare for intercourse. It's not nearly as serious as intercourse. For the most part you won't have the fears of pregnancy or STDs, the guilts, or the loss of self-esteem that you'd have with intercourse.

Of course, it will in part depend on how far you go in foreplay. Go too far and you'll be more and more tempted to go all the way. It might "just happen" before you can stop. If you play with fire too much, you just might get burned.

110 Will it harm you if you abstain from having sex?

Not one little bit. Unless you repress your sex urge completely, you will suffer no harm. Some people are quite satisfied to go without sex for long periods, or even their entire lives. And that's OK too.

111 What exactly is wrong with having premarital sex?

Having premarital sex involves a number of risks and decisions. Dr. Brent C. Miller has put these questions into a clear chart.

FIGURE 1. **Turning Points and Outcomes of Adolescent Pregnancy**[2]

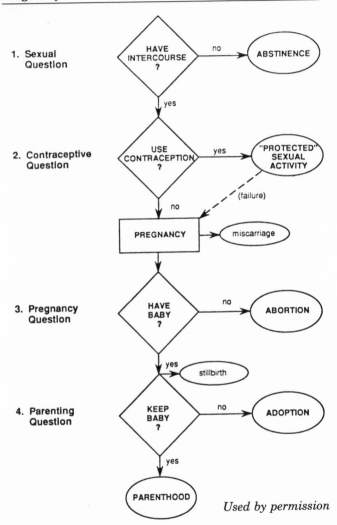

1. Sexual Question

2. Contraceptive Question

3. Pregnancy Question

4. Parenting Question

HAVE INTERCOURSE ?

no → ABSTINENCE

yes

USE CONTRACEPTION ?

yes → "PROTECTED" SEXUAL ACTIVITY

no

(failure)

PREGNANCY → miscarriage

HAVE BABY ?

no → ABORTION

yes

stillbirth

KEEP BABY ?

no → ADOPTION

yes

PARENTHOOD

Used by permission

112 **Is it wiser to have unwed sex or to abstain?**

That is the first question to settle in your own mind. What are the pluses? What are the risks?

The main advantages are (1) it may—though it may not—feel good while you are doing it; and (2) there is the good feeling of being close and cuddly with someone. Men are mostly more interested in, and satisfied by, the first. Women care more about the second. It may or may not be all that pleasing to her, especially at first.

But even if it is a great pleasure for both, it is only a brief joy. Studies show that couples in America have sex an average of about 1.1 times per week.[3] (We used to think it was 2-3 times.) Add to that the fact that each session lasts only eight minutes—foreplay, afterglow, and all. That means only about 10 minutes a week are spent enjoying sex.[4] Weigh that over against: the risks of getting pregnant; the chance of getting an STD such as AIDS; the risk of getting caught by parents, etc. The question you must ask yourself: Is the 10 minutes worth it?

Pretty tough questions. So what about both of you staying a virgin, or just not having sex?

113 **What does it mean to be a virgin?**

You are a virgin if you have not penetrated a vagina (male), or been penetrated in the vagina (female), by any person in sexual intercourse. The term is most often applied to females, but should equally apply to males.

Judging from the many, many questions I get from adolescents, there is still a lot of interest and concern about being a virgin. Here are some samples:

Am I still a virgin if . . .

I've had an orgasm without intercourse?	You are still a virgin.
I've had oral (mouth to genital) sex?	You are still a virgin.
I've had anal (penis to anus) sex?	You are still a virgin.
I've been fingered (in the vagina)?	You are still a virgin.
I've been penetrated by other than a penis?	You are still a virgin.
He tried, but could not penetrate?	You are still a virgin, but just barely. And it's not your fault that you still are.
I had intercourse, but did not have an orgasm?	You are not a virgin.
I had intercourse, but the guy did not enter all the way. Just a little.	You are not a virgin.

Some of the above cases are, by strict definition, still virgins. The vagina was not entered. But in some cases, such as oral or anal sex, that is almost as risky as vaginal intercourse. Better watch it if you want to keep your virginity.

114 What are the odds of a girl who is a virgin finding a boy who is a virgin?

Sorry to say, the odds aren't all that good. We still have a long way to go in this country to rid ourselves of that old double standard. But there are some out there. You will, of course, have to take his word for it. There's no way you can tell for sure.

And let's face it; he may lie to you. In one study, 47 percent of the men and 42 percent of the women admitted telling lies about their former sex life. Even more lied about having sex with a prostitute, homosexual acts, and the use of illegal drugs.[5]

115 Are those of us who have had premarital sex doomed? I mean, is there no chance for us to have a great marriage?

Of course there is. It just means that you must take extra care in choosing your mate. Now that you recognize the extra risks in premarital sex, that will help you to use greater caution.

In fact, even though you are no longer a biological virgin, you can still become a *psychological virgin*. How do you do that? You must stop having sex *right now*. Then the longer you go without having sex, the less its negative factors will affect you. You can then enter your marriage as a psychological virgin and share in the intimate joy of sex within a committed and loving marriage.

116 If persons have had premarital sex just once, but have abstained for several years, are their chances of successful marriage as good?

Yes, just about as good. They are now psychological virgins.

117 How do you tell your parents you aren't a virgin any more?

With great care! Most parents will be something less than ecstatic at that bit of news. Some dads may even boot you out. They may be very unhappy with you, but they may appreciate your honesty. They may take it better if you show regret, and assure them that you won't make the same mistake again.

118 Is virginity the best wedding gift you can give to your marital mate?

Indeed it is. It will be welcomed the most, and cost the least. And it will give you a wonderful feeling as well—and an even better feeling if your spouse can return the favor.

119 How can I stop having sex?

That won't be easy. It will take will power—or *won't* power. But if you really want to quit strongly enough, you can do it. Try to avoid situations where you will be tempted. Have a clear understanding with each person you date. Tell them nicely but firmly that you just aren't going to do that. After a while it will be easier. Go for it. You'll be glad you did. And remember. You can even become a psychological virgin.

120 Do we listen to the church or to science on questions of premarital sex?

This may come as a surprise, but you can listen to both. Science and the church come out at about the same place, though for quite different reasons. Since I'm a scientist as well as an ordained minister, perhaps I can shed some light on the question.

First, one thing should be made quite clear. We scientists are not in the business of telling you or anyone else what you should do. Our job is to give you facts. What you do with those facts is up to you. We don't preach at you.

121 How does having sex before you marry hurt your marriage?

Science has established eleven facts concerning the probable effect of premarital sex on your marriage.

FACT 1: *Premarital sex tends to break up couples.* Other things being equal, couples who engage in sex are more likely to break up before marriage than those who do not. So what about the young woman who gives in to sex in the hope that she won't lose her young man? ("I'm afraid if I don't give in, he'll cut out.") She would more likely *hold him* if she *holds out.* And if he does cut out—good riddance! If sex is all he wants, you are better off without him.

FACT 2.: *Many men and women do not want to marry a person who has had intercourse with someone else.* Some fellows do their level best to reduce the number of virgins in the population! Yet when it comes time to marry, they don't want a girl who's been pawed over by other guys. Their strange logic seems to be: "It's OK for me to have sex with the girl you marry, but it's not OK for you to have sex with mine."

In one Kinsey study, over half the college-level males under age 25 expected to marry a virgin, or at least a woman who had had sex with no one else. That proportion may since have changed, but many women as well as men still secretly hold that hope. In fact, in a more recent survey of young men chosen for listing in *Who's Who Among High School Students,* almost two out of three (63 percent) said they prefer to marry a virgin.

Nor are men the only ones who prefer to marry a virgin. Recent studies show that for both sexes, the more sexual experience the other person has had, the less desirable that person is. This is true not only for the choice of mates, but also for dates. And it applies to those who have had oral sex or same-sex experience as well. Both sexes prefer partners who have done no more than moderate petting— breast, or at most, genital fondling.[6]

Fear of AIDS is another factor now. A study published in 1991 showed that nearly one-third of the sexually active [unmarried] U.S. women claim they have altered their sex life in some way as a result of the AIDS threat. And 80 percent of them take into account their chances of getting HIV.[7]

FACT 3: *Those who have premarital sex tend to have less happy marriages.* On the whole, your chances of being happily married are better if you wait till you're wed to have sex. And the more premarital sex you have, the less likely you'll be happy in your marriage.

FACT 4: *Those who have premarital sex are more likely to have their marriage end in divorce.* This follows from Fact 3. If a couple is unhappy with their marriage, they're more likely to break up. And again, the more premarital sex the individuals have had, the greater the chance of divorce. It seems to make good sense to choose a one and only, "till death do us part."

FACT 5: *Persons and couples who have had premarital sex are more likely to have extramarital affairs.* One Kinsey report showed that women who had sex before marriage were *more than twice* as likely to cheat on their husbands as women who were virgins at the time of their marriage. This is even more true of men. The more premarital sex a person has had, the more likely he or she is to commit adultery.

This should come as no surprise. Take these cases. Suppose after marriage one meets a person one used to date and have sex with. He meets the gal on a business trip. Or she has lunch with the guy. It could be all very innocent. But if the couple has had sex with each other before, are they more likely or less likely to end up in bed together than if they had not had sex with each other before? I'll give you three guesses and the first two don't count!

Of course, once a couple have had sex with each other, it is much, much easier to do the same thing again, married or not. This factor may well be the most serious consequence of all for a marriage. Few wives, and even fewer husbands, are able to tolerate—much less approve—acts of adultery on the part of their spouse. Even in cases where it never gets discovered by the spouse, suspicions may well drive a deep wedge between the couple.

FACT 6: *Having premarital sex may fool you into marrying a person who is not right for you.* As we have seen, sex can blind you. You may believe you've found real love, when in fact it is only sex that has held you together. Since your sex is good, you may think your marriage will be. If you wait for sex until you're quite sure you have a sound relationship *without* sex, you can avoid this mistake. Once your good relationship is firmly established, then your married sex life becomes a beautiful, wondrous bonus. It will tie you together even more completely in your marriage.

The next two facts are best taken together. The first is a short-term plus, but the second a long-range minus.

FACT 7: *Persons and couples with premarital sex experience tend to achieve sexual satisfaction sooner after they are married. However . . .*

FACT 8: *They are likely to be less satisfied overall with their sex life during marriage.* That is, they adjust to sex more quickly, but their overall sex life is less satisfying.

Why should sexually experienced persons be less satisfied with their married sex life? One reason is that their premarital sex experience can rise to haunt them. Suppose that a certain wife has an orgasm about half the time when she and her husband have intercourse. She never has more than one climax during coitus. This means she is well above the national average, since only 30 percent of U.S. women have orgasms each time there is penetration.[8]

But what if the man she marries has had sex with other partners who had orgasms more? Isn't he likely to compare his wife's sexual "performance" with that of his previous partners? And so will the wife if she has had sex with other men. They can scarcely avoid such comparisons.

Now suppose that this same woman is married to a man who, like herself, has had sex with no one else. The only sex they have known is with each other. Are they not much more likely to be fully satisfied with the sex life they share? What they have is good, so they're happy with it. The statistics are clearly on their side.

Married sex is best. No matter how skilled and exotic and explosive a merely physical sexual experience may be, it cannot begin to match what I call "total sex." Total sex involves the completion and conjoining of total personalities. It merges the minds, the emotions, and the social and spiritual selves of a couple, as well as their two bodies. The two truly do become one. They can actually be worshiping God in the act of having sex. Why would any sensible person want to settle for anything less than that kind of sex?

FACT 9: *Poor premarital sexual habits can be carried over to spoil sex in marriage.* Sadly enough, this happens a lot. Kinsey studies found that more than half of U.S. wives are in some degree either not willing or not able to share sex freely and fully with their husbands. They have guilts and fears. They are hesitant or inhibited. The new 1990 Kinsey report confirms that a good many false ideas are still out there. Many wives—and to a lesser extent their husbands—have poor attitudes about sex even now, according to the new Kinsey reports.[9]

Why is this so? A number of reasons are often cited. Some in our society still cling to some early Victorian prudery about sex. Then, too, many Christians have adopted St. Paul's view that sex is "of the flesh" and hence to be shunned. They believe it is at best something that is not quite nice. Poor sex education in home, church, and school has been the rule. And unhealthy attitudes have been handed down by our elders. In all, we do have lots of "hang-up hangovers" from the past.

But in addition to these more familiar reasons for lack of sexual enjoyment, there is one factor that has escaped the attention it deserves. What is this culprit? It is *pre-marital intercourse,* along with other guilt-producing sex acts. Here's how that works.

Since premarital sex is still a social and religious no-no, illicit sex acts usually produce some degree of guilt, fear, and loss of self-esteem. This can apply to both partners, but it is especially true for women. They feel guilt, since they are doing what they feel they should not do. They lose self-respect, since they are not living up to their own ideals. And they are afraid of three things: getting caught in the act of sex, getting pregnant, and perhaps contracting an STD.

So what may happen if you get into premarital sex? Whether you're engaged or not, each time you have sex, you feel guilt and fear and loss of self-respect. Over and over again this happens. You have sex, you feel fear and guilt and remorse. In time, all of these negative feelings become associated with the sex act itself. You learn to tie sex with negative feelings.

Now suppose you do get married. Once wed, you have no further need to feel guilt, fear, and remorse when you engage in sex. Once you have that piece of paper, you have social license to have just about any kind of sex you choose. So as soon as the ceremony is over, you will suddenly be able to forget all about the past—right? You can fall into your spouse's arms on the honeymoon and be utterly uninhibited—right? You will shed all that backlog of guilt, fear, and shame like a snake sheds its skin in summer—right?

Wrong! To the extent you learned to associate sex with guilt and fear and shame *before* the wedding, you will in some measure feel that way *afterward.* So when you have sex, that guilt and fear and shame will come back to haunt you. It may take months or even years for you to recondition yourselves. Only then can your sex life be full and free.

FACT 10: *Guilt may push a couple into a bad marriage.* Many persons (especially those with a deep religious faith or background) will feel that they should have sex only with the person they wed and no one else. So they may feel duty-bound to marry a person they have had sex with. As a result, this guilt and sense of duty may push them into a poor marriage.

For instance, let's assume that a couple feel certain that they are in love. They get engaged. "Since we will soon marry anyway," they reason, "we'll just fudge a bit and start having sex." (A risky plan, remember, since one of every three engaged couples breaks up without marrying.) But later one or both develop some doubts. "Maybe this isn't love after all. Maybe we ought to break up." That would be the smart thing to do. But since they have already shared the sex, they feel obliged to go ahead with the wedding anyway—with sad results.

It happens a lot more often than most people think.

FACT 11: *Premarital sex robs a couple of "sexual cement."*[10] The sex act is the most intimate of all human behaviors. It bonds a couple together in a unique way. It is so wonderful that it keeps them coming back to each other for sex. They ignore severe problems in their relationship such as money, in-laws, etc.

I call this bonding "sexual cement," since it is so strong that it can hold a couple together for up to three to five years. Here's why it is of vital importance to hold off having sex until after you're wed. If you do, it can help you make your marriage a success.

This is how it works.

Two things we know. First, *the roughest period of adjustment for a couple in their marriage is the first five years.* That's when most divorces occur. The curve looks like this:

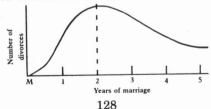

The peak problem years are the very first three. Now let's look at the second thing we know.

The peak of sexual excitement and thrill of having intercourse occurs in most cases in the very first year that a couple starts to have sex with each other. That curve looks like this:

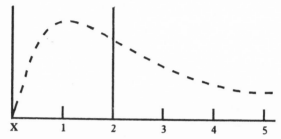

The very peak of their sexual thrills will likely occur in the very first year, followed by a gradual decline. After five years it has tended to level out so that sex becomes only one of many very important things to hold the couple together.

Now let's do some comparing. Suppose the couple begin having sex two years before they marry. Putting one curve over the other, we get:

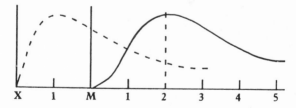

Right when the couple need it most to help them over the very roughest years of adjustment in their marriage, much of that wonderful sexual cement has already been spent.

How sad! One of the most powerful bonding forces available to any newlyweds has already lost a large portion of its thrilling appeal. That precious bonding of sex that could have helped hold them together while they worked out their problems has been largely lost.

But what if the couple do wait until marriage to have their first sexual intercourse? Again putting the two curves together, we get:

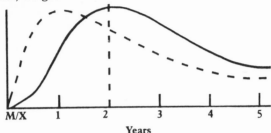

Years

Right when they need it most, they have those wondrous first years of their sex life to keep them coming back together until they can work out their problems and save their marriage. What a wonderful asset sex can be!

Now let's sum up the 11 known facts about sex before marriage. Other things being equal, if you have premarital sex you are more likely to:

1. Break up before you marry.

2. Scare off anyone who wants to marry a virgin.

3. Be less happy in your marriage.

4. Get a divorce.

5. Commit adultery after you marry.

6. Be fooled into marrying for the wrong reasons.

7. Achieve married sex happiness quicker, *but*

8. Be less satisfied with your married sex life.

9. Spoil total sex due to sexual salivation.

130

10. Have guilt feelings that may nudge you into a poor marriage.

11. Be deprived of that all-important "sexual cement" right when you need it the most.

It is not only significant *whether* you have premarital sex, but also *how much* you have. The more of it you have, the greater the impact of these 11 facts on your marriage.

It also matters *with whom* you have premarital sex. If you have sex only with the person you marry, Facts 1, 9 and 11 still apply to you. But for the most part the other seven facts apply less harshly than if you have sex with other persons as well.

122 Is premarital sex a sin?

Yes, your religion likely considers it so. Why is the church so strongly opposed to sex before marriage? Every major religious body in the U.S. today not only opposes but condemns premarital sex. I know of no exception. Christians—Catholics, Protestants, and Mormons, as well as Jews—all strongly oppose such behavior. They must have good reasons—and they do.

First of all, each of these groups puts great stock in their Scriptures. Most of them think that much or all of it is the inspired Word of God. So they oppose premarital sex because it is so strongly condemned in these Scriptures.

Look at the facts. The big word for premarital sex in the Bible is *fornication*. I traced that word through 11 major Bible concordances or dictionaries.* That word, or some form of it, is used at least 56 times. It appears all the way from Genesis right on through Revelation. In every single place it is used it is strongly condemned as a great sin.

*For these sources, see Appendix 1.

In the Old Testament period, sex outside of marriage was on a par with being a harlot, a whore, or "unfaithful." Was it frowned upon in the Bible? Just look at the penalty for those caught doing it. In some cases both parties were to be stoned to death (Deut. 22:21-29; John 8:5). Capital punishment, no less! Scarcely the penalty for a minor crime. At the very least, a man who had sex with a virgin was forced to pay a stiff fine to her father. Then he had to marry the girl, *with no chance ever to divorce her.* That must have cooled the ardor of a lot of guys on the prowl!

St. Paul listed fornication in the same class with serious sins like adultery and murder (Rom. 1:29; Gal. 5:19). So did Jesus (Mark 7:21-22). The church today continues to share Paul's dim view of sex outside of marriage.

But not all religious groups oppose sex out of marriage *just* because the Bible is against it. They see that such actions hurt people in many ways. They see marriages being destroyed when one partner cheats. They bleed for the plight of the unwed mother. They feel pity for the child who is born unplanned, unwanted, unrespected, rejected, and neglected. They know the misery of those who have bodies riddled and broken with sexually transmitted disease. They see the tragedy of people who just use other people for their own selfish ends. They know how guilt and fear and low self-regard can rob a person of the good life.

In sum, the evil that can result seems much too high a price to pay for the thrill of the moment that illicit sex may bring. Neither the church nor the Bible are against sex. Make no mistake about that. They are just against having sex until or unless a person can and will take full responsibility for the act.

123 How can I say "no" when the couple in the back seat is making out?

What goes on in the back seat is not your affair (pun intended). Your concern must be with what goes on in the front seat. Don't let peer pressure push you into trouble.

Often "the gang" may urge you to do what you know you shouldn't do. Then if you get in trouble, they cut out. They leave you in the lurch.

So before giving in to peer pressure—and it can be really rough at times—think it through. Will *they* pay the price if you get caught, or will *you?* If they dare you to steal, will they serve your jail term? If you get drunk, will they take the flack? If you get pregnant, will they pay the doctor bills? It's a good bet you'll be squarely on your own. So make your own choices.

In fact, when peers are pressing you to go against your own best judgment or your moral values, turn these very questions right back to them. Ask them right out: "Will you or won't you pay the piper for me?" Then be on your guard against being lied to.

And if the pressure gets too great, you might want to consider finding some new friends with values more like your own.

124 I hear sex is so much fun. Won't I be missing out on a whole lot of life if I put off having sex until I get married?

You are quite right on one point. Sex can and should be fun. It can be wonderful and exciting. It feels good. Of course it does. God made us that way for a good purpose. It keeps the human race from dying out.

Yes, sex can be fun and fine and fulfilling. But there's one strange thing about sex. *It's the only major human drive that we do not have to satisfy.* No person *has* to have sex. We can live perfectly normal, happy lives without it. Who ever heard of a person dying from lack of sex? People die of hunger. People die of thirst. Some die from heat or from cold. Some even die from lack of love. But I don't know of a single case on record where a person has died from lack of sex. Sex isn't a required course; it's an elective. You can take it, or leave it alone.

As to "missing out" if you wait for sex, that all depends on what you want out of life. Do you just want to have sexual pleasure for the moment? Or do you want long-range fulfillment in life? If you settle for present pleasures, you may pay an awful price for your fleeting fun, both now and in years ahead.

Even if you think you love your sex partner, you'll still be taking a whole list of reckless risks. Here are a few questions to ask yourself before you decide to have sex before you marry:

▶ Are my sex partner and I willing and able to face up to a pregnancy *right now?*

▶ What would a pregnancy do to our lives now? To plans each of us has for our future? (Only slightly more than half of the pregnant teenagers go on to get their high school diplomas.)[11]

▶ Am I really ready to be a parent now, or would I miss out on a lot of important things? Would I be forced to grow up too fast? Do I want to stay home and change diapers while my peers are having fun at parties?

▶ What would an unwed pregnancy do to my parents and other loved ones? My friends? Schoolmates? Do I want them to suffer with me?

▶ What about my pastor, teachers, and people in my church or club? How would it affect all those I care about, and those who care about and believe in me?

▶ Do I want a forced marriage?

125 What if a couple gets married and then finds that their sex organs don't fit?

They will fit just fine. Don't worry one bit about that. Any two human beings can have sex, be they tall or short, fat or skinny, black or white or purple.

Some women fear that the husband's penis will be too long or too large. It won't be. Studies show that erect penises are all about the same size. The variations are slight and not likely to cause problems.

The 1990 Kinsey Institute study reports that the average length of the erect male penis is 5 to 7 inches. There are very few variations. And even so, studies show that women for the most part don't have a preference in penis size.[12] In those rare cases where they are concerned, it is more likely because they fear it is too big. But even if a penis should be only 2 inches long, that will be long enough. That male will be able to have sex and make his wife pregnant just fine. No need to worry.

There's a simple reason why some men get the idea their penis is too big or too small. This is because, in a flaccid or soft condition, male penises vary a great deal in size. Sometimes they're scarcely more than a button. You may have to look twice to be sure he's a *he*. At other times they're almost as large as they are during an erection. The flaccid size varies widely between males, or at different times in the same male.

As to the female vagina being too small, those fears are just as groundless. The vagina's inner walls are flexible folds of flesh. They can stretch a very long way in almost every direction. In fact, just recall the size of a newborn baby's head and shoulders. That baby can come out of the same opening into which the male penis is inserted. No man alive should give a woman a problem!

In the relaxed, secure atmosphere of marriage, and with a normal amount of loving foreplay, there should be no barrier at all. If there is, see a doctor or counselor.

126 **I want to date a guy, and he wants to date me. He was previously living with a girl. Does that necessarily mean that he'll be expecting the same kind of favors from me?**

You guessed it! Studies show that the person who has gone all the way in sex in one relationship expects to go all the way in the next. So if you decide to date him, be prepared. You will no doubt be put under a lot of pressure to have sex.

By the way, the same pattern holds true with any level of necking and petting. He or she will tend to move quickly to that same level the next time. That is the case with the same person or with the next person he or she goes with. That's why it's so important not to go too far in the first place, no matter how much you think you're in love. It's a lot like "trying out" drugs or cigarettes. Once you start, it's very hard to stop. You get "hooked."

To conclude, here are a few facts about the frequency of teen sex and their number of partners. After they had their first sex, over two-thirds had it again within the next six months. Even most of the victims of forced sex went on to have voluntary sex during their teen years.

But here's the scary part. About four percent of the white females and 11 percent of the white males reported six or more partners during the past year. Shades of AIDS!

On the other hand, among the youth in their late teens, most had zero or just one partner in the past year. And unmarried teens were only about one-fourth as sexually active as their married counterparts.

Once you start having sex, it's tough to quit. Isn't it far better not to start in the first place? But if you've been into sex, and then quit, you can become a psychological virgin and gain back much of what you've lost. Remember: Sex is a joy; it's not a toy.

PART 10

The Problem of Pregnancy

127 I'm pregnant and don't know what to do. Can you help me?

You gambled—and lost. You chose having sex over abstinence.

You thought it just couldn't happen to you. But it did.

You thought the birth control method you chose—if you chose any at all—would work. It didn't.

So now you have only two options. Neither seems very attractive. You can have the baby, or have an abortion. We'll consider the pros and cons of each choice later in this chapter.

But first let's find out how widespread this problem is.

128 Is the adolescent pregnancy problem all that great, or are people just trying to scare us young people into not having sex?

Most older adults and professionals think it's scary, all right. That's not without good cause. Just look at the facts.

As early as the late 1970s, adolescent pregnancy cases began to rise at epidemic proportions in the United States. By 1988, we led the developed countries of the world in rates of early pregnancies, births, and abortions. And it keeps getting worse.[1] Now about seven percent of all U.S. women aged 15–17 get pregnant every single year.

I'd say those facts are scary. What do you think?

It becomes even more scary when we review the effects of early sex. The earlier a young person begins to have sex, the more likely these three things are true: (1) they are less likely to use birth control; (2) they are more likely to get a pregnancy they don't want; and (3) they are more likely to become a parent sooner than they are able to handle it well.[2]

Now let's have a look at the options open to the single woman who is pregnant.

129 Is it better to have the baby or have an abortion?

This choice is far from easy. First, let's look at the options:

Abortion means purposely ending a pregnancy before birth. About 80 percent of adolescent pregnancies are not intended. About half of these women choose to abort. Over one-fourth of these pregnant women used no birth control at all. Of those who did use it—and this is a surprise—55 percent did so with a parent's knowledge.[3]

Unmarried females are five times more likely to have an abortion as married ones. Unmarried Catholic women are about as likely to get an abortion as women in general do. This no doubt reflects the fact that the Vatican in Rome frowns on all forms of birth control except the rhythm method, which is quite risky. Also, one in six who get abortions described themselves as born again or evangelical Christians.[4]

130 Are abortions safe?

That depends. If it is a "back alley" abortion using a coat hanger, it is *most* unsafe. Many women have bled to death as a result. Yet the back alley type often happens when abortion is not legal. But if abortion is legal and available from trained medical professionals, it is quite safe for the mother. Of course, it's not safe for the fetus!

Now let's look at the other option.

Giving birth. Over 95 percent of the adolescents who give birth now keep their babies. If they do, look at what happens. They are more likely to:

▶ Have inadequate prenatal care while pregnant

▶ Give birth to low-weight babies

▶ Drop out before finishing high school, hence

▶ Earn low wages

▶ Have less spacing between births

▶ Have more babies

▶ End up on public welfare at taxpayers' expense[5]

And what about the children? They don't fare so well, either. They are more likely to (1) fail in school, (2) abuse alcohol and drugs, and (3) in general, have more behavior problems.[6]

Young women who are pregnant or have recently given birth are especially at risk of becoming homeless. That is even more likely to happen if the woman is under age 18.[7]

So you be the judge. Are adults just trying to scare young people, or is there real cause for their concern?

131 If you are an adolescent and give birth to a baby, is it better to keep the child or choose adoption?

Again, that depends on several factors. Most marriage and family scientists think it is better in most cases to give the child up for adoption. Most agree that this course is best for the baby. It is much better for a baby to grow up with two loving parents than just one. Unless the father of the child marries her, that will not be the case if she keeps the baby. In many states she is not allowed to see the baby or meet the adopting parents. That's rough on any mother, teen or not.

Of course, it is extremely hard for a young mother to give up her baby. She has felt its movements in her body. She has given birth through much pain. To then hand it over to others—often strangers—to rear, is no easy task. That's one reason why fewer than five percent of adolescent mothers go the adoption route.

There are interesting contrasts between those who choose adoption and those who keep their baby. Placers are more likely to have good life outcomes by age 30 in education, type of work, marital success, and finances. Other differences include:[8]

Life Factors	*Placers*	*Keepers*
Public assistance	4%	60 + %
Regrets over decision	more	less
Comfortable with her decision	more so	less so
Likely to go back to school	more	less
Hopes for post-high school education	3.3 yrs	2.1 yrs
Number married after birth of baby	3%	10%
Satisfied with their life	more	less
Good relations with her mother	more	less
Baby's mother/father may reclaim baby	more	less

These are some facts and likely results. They might be of help to any woman facing the tough choices she'll have if she gets pregnant.

132 Can a girl get pregnant if she goes swimming in a pool right after a couple have sex there?

I doubt that. If it ever happened I never heard of it. And by the way, that is one strange place to have sex!

133 Can a virgin girl get pregnant when having sex the first time?

You better believe it. Any time sperm gets into her vagina after she begins to ovulate, she can get caught.

134 Can you get pregnant if you have oral sex and swallow the semen?

Definitely not. There's no such thing as a pregnancy in the throat or stomach.

Swallow the semen? I guess it won't do you any harm. But don't you think there are better ways to get your protein? Besides that, with STDs around, you may get more than semen in the deal.

135 Can middle school kids have sex and get pregnant?

Yes on both counts. I sometimes wish kids that age couldn't have sex, but they can. A girl in Wisconsin was pregnant at age 11.

A final question. Which of the following two women was the smartest? Both came to my office at the University of Wisconsin—Platteville.

One of my former students got married and came by with her spouse. The couple were simply overjoyed. She was going to have a baby! He was so proud. Parents were delighted. Friends gave her baby showers. Everyone was extremely happy. And so was I. Bless their hearts, they're going to have a baby.

The second young woman was utterly distraught. "My God, Prof," she blurted out through her tears, "I'm going to have a baby. What am I going to do?" On the fifth date she had her very first intercourse, and got pregnant. She was full of anger and despair. Her parents were distressed and forced the reluctant boy to marry her. She cried out to me in anguish: "I don't want this baby! I don't want to be married! I don't want to be pregnant!" She was so miserable and disturbed that I feared she might commit suicide when she left my office.

Which young woman would you rather be? One was overcome with joy at being pregnant. The other would have given anything in the world if she had not been carrying that fetus. She hated being pregnant.

The choice is yours. You can either postpone sex so you can experience the joy of the first woman. Or you can engage in sex and risk being caught up in turmoil and stress like the second one.

PART 11

Does Birth Control Control Births?

If one is foolish enough to have premarital sex in spite of all the risks, that is one thing. But to be into sex without trying to avoid tragedy is even more foolish. It's just plain dumb!

Still, it is now clear that, like it or not, large numbers of adolescents do have sex. We have seen that about 90 percent of our youth have had sex by their 19th birthday. Our teen pregnancies in the United States outrun those in any other industrial country. We are number 1![1]

Given those facts, it is wise to do our best to help teens protect themselves from their own folly.

136 Why is the rate of teen pregnancy so high now?

Why so high? Well, they take the risks and many get caught.

As of now, only one out of five teenage couples who is sexually active takes the proper steps to guard against pregnancy. In fact, one out of three teen girls who has sex gets pregnant outside of marriage. (One in five of these gets pregnant within the first month after she starts having sex.[2] She doesn't even get to enjoy sex very much before her world comes crashing down.)

The question a girl must ask, then, is not, "Good grief, what would I do *if* I got pregnant?" She should ask instead, "What will I do *when* I get pregnant?" The second question is more to the point—and a lot more sobering.

Most teenagers just do not take the proper care to hold down the risks. Only about 50 percent of U.S. females use any kind of birth control at all the first time they have sex.[3] Such neglect spells trouble. Why? Because adolescents who do not use birth control at first intercourse are four times as likely to get pregnant as those who do.[4]

137 Is it true that the pill does not work as well when teenagers use it? If that is true, why is it so?

It is true, all right. Over 10 percent of teen pill users got pregnant in the first year of use.

Part of the reason is that they just forget to take it daily. Since most keep it a secret from their folks, there's no one to help remind them. They're on their own—and forget to remember.

Furthermore, one must read at 10th-12th grade level in order to follow the directions on the package. But on average, U.S. students read at one grade level below their actual grade. Hence, many teen pill users just can't understand the instructions. What is the best thing for her to do if she misses a day? Or two? Or more? She just won't know, so she guesses—and goofs.[5] One teen wondered why in the world she got pregnant. She was simply furious. "How could that have happened?" she fumed. "I took one of those pills every single month!" Hm-m-m. How indeed!

After they start to have sex, teenagers often wait a year or more to go to a family planning clinic for birth control help.[6] One study found that the first visit to a doctor or clinic after first sex was 23 months. That is extremely risky. Married couples who take no precautions at all will likely conceive on average about the eighth month.

144

138 Why are U.S. teens so slow to use contraceptives?

There are many factors. Here's some of them:

1. They won't admit they are, or may become, sexually active.

2. They don't know what kind of sex can lead to pregnancy.

3. They don't know what methods can help cut the risks.

4. They refuse to admit that it can happen to them.

5. They are too embarrassed or shy to go for birth control help.

In order to improve the situation, teens must:

1. Feel strongly that pregnancy would be a very negative thing.

2. Realize that the great costs of pregnancy—social, financial, psychic, etc.—outweigh the risks of conceiving.

3. Recognize that they may need to negotiate with their partner and agree on what method to use.

4. Know they must review often their risks and options.[7]

139 Which teens are more likely to use effective birth control?

Studies by scientists show that the teens who are more likely to use contraceptives are those who:

1. Are older and hence more likely to be more mature.

2. Have the money and transportation to get good contraceptives.

3. Know how and where to obtain them.

4. Plan their first sex, not have it "just happen."

5. Have more stable relationships.

6. Have school success, high goals in education, and good chances of achieving those goals.

7. Are more aware of the risks involved.

8. Are convinced of the disadvantages of getting pregnant.

9. Are not likely to get an abortion if they do get caught.

10. Are not deterred by the disadvantages of birth control or by the embarrassment in getting them.

Teens who live in poverty are much less likely to use effective methods. They may not have the funds to buy them or know how or where to get them. Also they tend to get less education and to have more limited goals for themselves. And they may lack the funds to pay for other forms of fun.[8]

These lists of facts may seem a bit overwhelming to some readers. But it is important to know what factors lead sexually active teens to use—or not use—protection against diseases and pregnancy. Knowing these facts can help us to predict which teens are most at risk and then help them reduce those risks. Clearly, their best choice is not to have unwed sex. But if they refuse to refrain? Then the next best course is to help them get some protection from possible tragedy, or even death.

For those persons who did use some form of birth control at first intercourse, what did they choose to use? Their first choice was the condom. Second, the pill. Third, withdrawal. One note of interest. Fundamentalist Protestants were less likely to use any form of birth control than were other Protestants or Catholics.[9]

We now turn attention to the various methods of birth control. Some are quite effective, others are far from it.

140 If you are sexually active, what would you suggest as the best protection? What about the condom?

The *condom,* commonly called rubber, is the only method that gives any protection at all from both pregnancy and sexually transmitted diseases (STDs). That includes the HIV virus which brings on AIDS. Only latex condoms give any shield against HIV, since this virus is 17 times smaller than a male sperm. Animal condoms give no protection at all from HIV.

Even with latex condoms, one study found that 16 to 33 percent of them leaked the HIV virus—even if they did not break.[10] Two recent tests have been made on large numbers of various brands. One of the tests was by Consumer's Union. In one test, one type of a highly advertised brand leaked HIV 100 percent of the time. But some were highly dependable.[11]

The condom is sometimes called a "safe," but it's a long way from being safe. Former U.S. Surgeon General C. Everett Koop reported that one out of five condoms sold in America leak. That is only 80 percent "safe." Another study found that about one in seven condoms (14.6 percent) either broke or slipped off the penis. That results in full exposure for both partners.[12] This means a disturbing level of risk, even for those who do use condoms.

And are you ready for this? When teenagers use the condom it is not 80-85 percent effective, but only 45 percent!

141 Why are condoms so ineffective when used by teens?

For one thing, most teens don't get the best condoms. They shrink from going to Planned Parenthood (someone may think they are arranging an abortion). They fear that the local pharmacist who fills the family prescriptions may squeal to their parents. So where do they get them? Out of a slot machine in the john of a truck stop.

Now the trick is: How do we keep mom and dad from finding out? So they pack them around in their billfold—in a hip pocket—all rolled up, hoping they'll get a chance to use them. Since billfolds are flexible, the condom gets wear. Where? Right on the end where there must not be any wear.

Also, body heat can weaken the latex. And the heat in a glove compartment can be even worse. Then if an oil product like Vaseline or baby oil is used as a lubricant, worse yet. Such products can produce holes in 60 seconds big enough for HIV to pass through. Shortly after that, there are holes that sperm can wriggle through.[13] Also, the high ozone levels often found in urban smog causes exposed condoms to deteriorate rapidly.[14]

So guess what: only 45 percent. Some jaws really drop when I drop that little pearl in a high school assembly.

There is one further problem. Even the best of condoms are no good unless they get used. Yet teen males who have the most risky kind of sex seem least likely to use condoms. This includes teen males who (1) had sex most often, (2) had more partners, (3) had already contracted an STD, and (4) used alcohol or cocaine.[15]

142 Is a *female condom* more effective than a male condom?

No, it is rated 85 percent, or about the same. However, over half of the users of these condoms were not satisfied with them.[16]

143 How safe is *the pill?*

For most women it is quite safe. However, those who are heavy smokers or have certain liver problems should never take the pill. In such cases, it could even be fatal. That is too bad because women who smoke or drink or do drugs are the very ones more likely to have sex and get pregnant. Also, girls should have six months to one year of regular menstrual flow before going on the pill.[17]

There is another danger. Women on the pill are about 70 percent more likely to get infected with chlamydia and gonorrhea than women who are using an IUD (intrauterine device) or who are sterilized. Pill users are also four times as likely as nonusers to have abnormal cervical tissue growth. That could lead to cancer.[18]

And by the way. Cervical pre-cancer is over twice as likely in women who smoke cigarettes. And the more they puff, the more the risk. Women who have had three or more sex partners have twice the risk as well. The chances are also greater if young women had their first sex before age 18.

Is Mother Nature trying to tell us something? Maybe high moral standards do pay off after all.

One more tragic danger. The pill offers no protection at all against catching the AIDS virus. Only a condom does that. But while 30 percent of teen pill users are at high risk for getting STDs, only 16 percent also use a condom during sex.[19]

Fully 23 percent of all pill users have not graduated from high school. Some urban teen pill users have a failure rate of up to 20 percent.[20]

144 **How effective are the birth control implant in the woman's arm and other forms of birth control?**

The *Norplant* is the best protection from pregnancy of all the methods—99 percent or better (except saying NO, which is 100 percent). It gives no protection at all from STDs or AIDS. The small rods, about the size of a match stick, can be removed at any time pregnancy is desired.

It works in a similar way as the pill, except that you don't have to remember to take it. It, like the pill, fools your body into thinking you are pregnant. There may be side effects similar to pregnancy. At least at first. But it works as well with teenagers as with anyone else.

The life-long side effects have yet to be determined, since Norplant hasn't been around here that long. An implant that gradually dissolves is now being tested but is not yet approved in the United States as of this writing.

The *IUD*—intrauterine device—is rated in the 98 to 99 percent range for birth control. Just like every other method except the condoms, protection against AIDS and STDs is zero. Zilch. None.

This small gadget is placed inside the uterus and is left there until removed. One type produced so many problems—even some deaths—that the company that made it was driven into bankruptcy by law suits. But other types are now making a comeback here. The *diaphragm* is a barrier method used by women. If she is fit with the right size and uses it with a spermicide, it gives about 85 percent protection from pregnancy. But again, none from

STDs. Once the best method medics could give, it is now seldom used.

Spermicides used by themselves or with *sponges* are only about 75 percent effective. As the names imply, they kill or impede the sperm. They are better than nothing at all, but still plenty risky.

145 Can the timing method of birth control work?

Fertility awareness is the term now in vogue. It's often called the rhythm or "safe period" method. But it usually isn't very safe. It is only about 75 percent effective. Failure rates range from 16 to 30 percent. The theory is that a woman can conceive only about 14 days before onset of her next menstrual period.

But that just is not true. Many women ovulate at quite unexpected times—even during menstruation—so says the new Kinsey report. Presence of an ovum can be affected by having a cold or the flu or by sudden stress or other disruptions.[21] Further, we now know that sperm may live in a woman's body for up to eight or nine days.[22]

The odds are much better if both partners have had a thorough study course on how best to make it work. But that means the couples can only have sex about 11 days each month. That is not the most popular idea around for most husbands—and some wives.

146 Are guys capable of holding their sperm when having sex?

Withdrawal is the usual name for this. In theory, the penis is taken out of the vagina before he ejaculates. But that method is a real bummer. It has a failure rate of about 23 percent—about one out of 4.[23]

Can he hold his sperm? Don't count on it. One reason for failure is that some men start to ejaculate before they think they have. Plenty of sperm to do the job are already injected. And don't forget. Even those little droplets of pre-ejaculate fluid contain live sperm 40 percent of the time. That is especially true if he has ejaculated in the recent past.

Add to that the fact that many men are not above lying to a woman about pulling out in time. The result is bad news. Right when he'd give his right arm not to have to leave is exactly when he's got to get out. He's likely to overstay his welcome. Don't trust withdrawal at all.

Douching (washing) out the vagina is not good news either. No matter what you use: water, vinegar or—would you believe—Coca Cola? For one thing, filling the vagina with a liquid may force more live sperm into the uterus than would swim there on their own. But more than that. Science has found that it takes only 20 seconds after sperm are ejaculated into the vagina for some of them to swim into the uterus. A woman has to be quite a sprinter to make it in time!

False notions about sex and pregnancy lead some teens to think they are safe. These next questions may sound silly, but the answers could save you from a poor choice. It's better to ask questions and learn the truth.

147 Is saran wrap as good as a condom?

NO! It has plenty of holes—more than enough. Furthermore, it tears very easily and gets displaced.[24] And it would be awfully awkward to cope with. What would hold it on, a rubber band? Or a twister?

Forget it. You might just as well use a hair net.

148 If the girl jumps up and down right after sex, will that decrease the chance of pregnancy?

You've got to be kidding! Sperm are mobile, remember? And they are strong. Those little guys can swim upstream. No, you might as well save the aerobics for gym class.

And doing it standing up won't help, either.

149 Why is it so easy for a girl to get pregnant?

Any time fresh live sperm get on the vulva or in the vagina, she can conceive. Sperm have tails. They can swim really well. And every one of them want to make a bee line for that ovum.

And get this. One study suggests that the ovum actually beckons the sperm right up to it. Some call that the "come hither" effect.[25] In this case, it's the female who whistles at the male!

It's hard to outsmart Mother Nature. If there is any way at all to get a woman pregnant, Mother Nature will find it.

150 If you use many types of birth control at once, does that help your chances of not getting pregnant?

Of course. You can make a big deal out of it. But if you go to all that trouble, you may want to ask yourself, "Is all this really worth it?" More than one condom may help, but after a while he may not even know what's going on. Wouldn't it be better to think in terms of just not doing it?

As one recent study notes, no one contraceptive now available is highly effective in protecting against both pregnancy and STD infection. To be safer, couples may have to use two methods at once.[26]

To sum it all up, no method of contraception is 100 percent effective. And only condoms give any protection against AIDS while having sex. The very best way to avoid both is abstinence. Better to wait and to refrain, than not to wait and bear the pain.

But if you insist on doing it, use your head as well as your tail, OK? Protection against STDs and AIDS *must* include the condom. The pill or implant or rhythm method or whatever may help avoid pregnancy. They are no help at all in avoiding sexual diseases.

PART 12

Can Boozer Choosers be Losers?

151 Some of my friends drink alcohol and put pressure on me to do the same. I don't want to do that. What should I do?

You are being smart not to yield to that pressure. For one thing, alcohol is a drug. Like cocaine, heroin, and other illegal drugs, it is habit-forming. You could become an addict and mess up your life now, and spoil your future.

Even so-called social drinkers are at risk. About one in 11 persons who drink will end up being an alcohol problem. It used to be one in 14. And as of now, we have no way of predicting which person it will be. If you start to drink, that person could well be you. If you don't drink at all, there is no way you can become a problem drinker. Or worse yet, an alcoholic.

152 Are parents who drink part of the alcohol problem? Are they setting a bad example?

A big part of the problem is that many parents themselves drink. That serves as an example for their young. Underage teens may reason: "If they do it, why can't I?" Most young teens like to think of themselves as grown-up, too. Of course, there is a difference. It is legal for older adults and not for you. Even so, older adults can drink and drive and have fatal accidents just like anyone else. And they do. The result is that a large number of fatal auto accidents involve a driver under the influence.

So even if you have parents who drink, it is not smart to sneak around and drink. They may drink and get by with it. You might not be so lucky.

A further word on peer pressure to drink. When I was a young man, something happened to me that could have changed my whole life. It could have put me in prison. Instead, it made a total abstainer out of me—to this very day.

One night in Idaho, I was driving home from a date. Now, in scarce water country, the roads normally go up over irrigation ditches. As I went over one such hump, my headlights came down on the road. There, lying right across the road, was a man!

I slammed on the brakes. Tires squealed. When I finally stopped, the front wheel of the car was just inches from the man's throat! One more foot and I would have killed my drunken neighbor, who had seven small children to support.

Now, scientists know that even small traces of alcohol in one's body will slow a person's reaction time. Even if I'd had just one drink—one lousy drink—I could not have stopped in time. It would have been a case of manslaughter. I have always been glad that I resisted the pressure to drink as a teenager. I think you will be, too, if you resist.

153 Just because we may drink once in a while as a teenager doesn't mean we will do it when we are older, does it?

It probably does. A high school classmate of mine used to get half drunk or worse at the drop of a cork. And 40 years later at a class reunion, guess what? He turned up snockered again. He got hooked in high school and now he's hooked for life—unless he gets help.

Patterns of behavior that we form in our youth tend to be a predictor of what we do later. The main point is that it's hard to judge the effects your adolescent actions will have on your later life. So why take the chance?

154 Is there any connection between using alcohol and drugs and getting into sex?

Yes, there is a clear connection. In one study, 94 percent of pregnant 17-year-olds had used alcohol. Also, 78 percent had used marijuana, often called "pot." And get this: 30 percent had used the hard stuff—cocaine.

Teens who are hard drug users are almost four times more likely to be at risk of getting pregnant, and five times as likely to have an abortion.

Those teens who began using these substances became sexually active soon after—within a year. This also applied to cigarette smoking. And the younger they are when they get involved in such behaviors, the younger both males and females get into sex.[1] Drug and alcohol use is also associated with getting into trouble with the law as delinquents.[2] Yes, it's all tied together.

155 Does smoking lead to sexual behavior?

Studies show that smoking is correlated with teens being active in sex, and getting pregnant unwed. We know that it causes diseases that kill people, such as lung cancer and emphysema. Further, we know that women who smoke get addicted more deeply than men. But does that stop women from smoking? Sadly enough, not at all. Of all women in the United States between the ages of 18 and 44, one in four smoke.[3]

And that's not all. Youth with low self-esteem are more likely to get into sex and drugs.

156 Am I being too harsh to want a husband who does not drink alcohol at all? I don't want to have any drinking or smoking in my home.

Too harsh? Sounds to me like you have good sense. Husbands who pop the cork are far more likely to beat up on their wives. And they do so more often. Furthermore, secondhand smoke has now been shown without question to be a serious health problem to all who inhale it.

Stick to your guns, lady. There are still good men out there who are smart enough to neither smoke nor drink. And there are a lot worse things in this world than being single.

157 Is it good to get a girl drunk before sex?

This sounds like a selfish, dirty trick. But there are guys who try to do it. Women ought to be on guard. Men say, "Aw, come on honey. Let's have another beer." Or, "Let's have just one more drink." One boy said he got a girl so drunk she passed out. "But no man would take advantage of a girl in that condition," he lied.

Alcohol tends to lead persons to lose their best judgment and moral values. Girls, beware!

Women who smoke and drink take many risks. They are twice as likely to have cervical pre-cancer if . . .

▶ they have had sex before age 18

▶ they have had more than three sex partners

▶ they are smokers—and the more cigarettes they smoke, the greater the risk.[4]

And women who are heavy smokers are over three times as likely to have a tubal (ectopic) pregnancy.[5]

PART 13

STDs: Those Antisocial Social Diseases

158 What are STDs and how do you get them?

Sexually transmitted diseases (STDs) have now reached more than epidemic levels among the young in the United States. And it is getting worse. Every 13 seconds a teenager gets an STD.[1]

Women are more likely to catch one from men than men are likely to catch one from women.

They are called STD because they are mainly spread by sexual contact. It is wise to avoid any activity that exposes you to the blood, semen, secretions of the vagina, menstrual blood, feces, or saliva of another person. These should be considered high risk. The one exception is if one is in an *exclusive relationship* with a partner who is proven not to be infected. You guessed it. I think that should be in marriage.

There are over 50—some say over 70—STDs that you can catch. Once you get one, you can get it again and again. Unlike with mumps and measles, your body does not build immunity to an STD.[2] And if you do get another STD, you are several times more likely to catch AIDS. Since AIDS is now always fatal, we'll take it up in a later chapter.

The highest risk of getting an STD is if one has unprotected vaginal or anal sex. If one does that, the only partial protection as of now, is to use condoms with a spermicide. It's far from perfect, but it's the best there is. Some condoms leak. Some break. Some slip off. Or areas not covered by the condom, such as the male scrotum, can pick up infection from an STD like genital herpes II. Of course, the only 100 percent protection is just not to have intercourse at all. That is, not until you find that one mate who is to be your sole sex partner for life.

In rare cases, an STD could be caught from objects like health spa benches or toilet seats. But this is highly unlikely. Some opening in your body or break in your skin would have to come in contact with a very recent discharge from someone who was contagious. Nurses have in fact been known to catch it from bed sheets. But this is so unlikely that the risk can safely be ignored. We don't have to go back to putting toilet paper on the seat before we sit down. But it might be wise to check for fresh moisture. The herpes II virus has been known to live for more than four hours outside the human body.

One nasty trait is common to most of these diseases. They hit and run. The outer symptoms, if they are visible at all, last only a brief while. Then they appear to disappear. The victims might breathe a sigh of relief. "Whew! That was close," they may say to themselves. But beware. Some STDs are tricky. Just because the symptoms are gone doesn't mean the disease has left. It has just gone underground. In some cases it may be doing severe, even deadly damage to the body, as we shall see.

159 If you get an STD, what will it do to you?

These are sometimes called social diseases. That's a laugh. They are in fact very *anti*social. Some kinds may not hurt you very much at first. In the case of gonorrhea, for instance, four out of five women (and some men) have no outward signs or symptoms at all. In women these clues may be inside the body and therefore not be detected. They may have it and spread it, yet never know they have it.

160 **What kinds of STDs are there?**

Several of them are more well known than others. You may have heard of syphilis, chlamydia, and human papilloma virus or genital warts.

Less well known perhaps is pelvic inflammatory disease (PID). It may have no obvious symptoms, but may rob a woman of her chances to have children. This one costs taxpayers a bundle. In 1990, the cost of PID and its consequences came to $4.2 billion. By contrast, the cost of treating a single case of chlamydia or gonorrhea was only $66.[3]

161 **If you get an STD, can it be cured?**

Most of them can be, but not all. This is one reason STDs are spreading so fast among the young. There are at least three of them that can't be cured. Get one of these and you will carry it to your grave. One of them will carry *you* to the grave. What are they?

1. *Gonorrhea,* the Asian strain. Like syphilis, this one is a germ. Scientists do pretty well at killing germs. We can now cure all the cases of syphilis and gonorrhea, even in late stages. But not the Asian strain. That one is penicillin resistant. The wonder drugs won't help. You get it, you just have to take it. And it isn't very nice.

It, too, is an STD that may make it so a woman can never, ever be able to have a baby of her own. The scar tissue plugs up the Fallopian tubes. It doesn't take much to plug them up. The inner opening of the tube is only a bit larger than a human hair. Once plugged, she can never conceive. What a price to pay for a few premarital sex thrills!

160

Regular gonorrhea has similar symptoms, but it can be cured. Gonorrhea is often called "clap." It is mainly found in young persons. Almost two out of three cases of gonorrhea occur in those under age 24. In men, within a week after catching it there is likely to be a discharge from the penis. The tip of the penis becomes swollen and inflamed.

In most men and in some women there's a frequent urge to urinate. But when they do, it stings and hurts. Left untreated, the male's testes may swell and cause pain. Gonorrhea can cause a person to go blind, get arthritis, and have heart, prostate, kidney, and many other physical problems.[4] It isn't very nice.

The place most women get infected is in the cervix (neck of the womb). External signs (in the 20 percent of cases where they do appear) include a vulva that gets red and raw and a discharge from the vagina. Since most women don't even know they have the disease, it goes untreated. Therefore complications occur more often and are more serious than with men. A woman's tubes and ovaries may get abscesses that require surgery. She may become an invalid or even die. Not a pretty picture, is it?

2. *Genital herpes II* is a second STD for which there is no known cure. Herpes I, its cousin, is harmless. It produces cold sores and we all get those. However, it can be spread by kissing, even via wet towels, washcloths, water glasses, cups, or toothbrushes.[5]

Genital herpes II can be spread easily, too. When the infected area is shedding, you can catch it almost as easily as you can catch a common cold. It can get into your mucous membranes, like the mouth, lips, throat, and of course, the sex organs. It can live as long as three days or more on things like towels, bed sheets, etc. It's possible, but not likely, that you can get it from a bathtub or toilet seat. But it is mainly spread by sexual activity.[6]

Like AIDS, it's a virus. Scientists have not been able to do much to cure viruses. For example, the common cold is a virus. We've tried for centuries to find a cure. We haven't found one yet.

So what will happen if you get herpes II? Since there is no known cure, it is spreading like wildfire. The same is true of that Asian strain of gonorrhea. If you get either one of these you will have to pay the price, and it may be a very dear one. Herpes II at first brings pain and itching. Then come fluid-filled sores and blisters.

3. *AIDS* is the deadly STD. An in-depth discussion is found in the next part of this book.

162 Can you get genital herpes other places?

In nine out of ten cases these sores occur around the genitals, though sometimes in and around the mouth. Scientists think it's being spread to the mouth by oral sex. These blisters can rupture into open sores. If they do, the pain can be most severe. One victim said every time she had to go to the bathroom, the pain was almost too great to bear. Another complained, "I thought I'd die. I couldn't lie down. I couldn't sit or bend over. I couldn't walk." I can't help wondering what in the world she did do!

Usually within about 20 days these sores get hard, scab over, and heal. One may think it is gone. But the end is not yet. At first, some people have it almost all the time. A new outbreak can come at any time, though often it may not be as severe. One woman had it recur every two weeks and last 10 days. Times of stress seem to help bring it on.

The effects of herpes can be tragic. The open sores may get infected. Cancer of the cervix is four times more likely in women with herpes II. A mother with an active case of herpes has a high risk of giving it to her baby as it is being born. Half of those babies will die, and half of the rest will suffer physical or mental damage. The only way to avoid that risk is a Caesarian section—delivering the baby by cutting open the mother's body.

And get this. Herpes may well mess up or even destroy your sex life. Over a third of male herpes victims experience impotence. That is, they are unable to perform or enjoy sex properly. A quarter of the victims felt destructive rage. One man became so angry that he vowed to spread it to as many women as he could. One woman bragged that she had given it to over 75 men, "to get even." And over half of those who had herpes gave up sex entirely, at least for a time. Herpes and other types of STD can be dangerous to your sex life! What a price to pay for a few risky sex thrills.

163 What are the chances and results of getting chlamydia?

Chlamydia has become the most common STD in the United States today. We now get about 4 million infections a year. That means your chances of getting it are very high indeed.

It often has no symptoms that one can detect, especially in women. Still it can do serious damage. It can lead to tubal pregnancy, which is very dangerous. It can deprive a woman of her chance to have babies of her own. And it can give a person chronic pain.

In spite of its rapid spread, the U.S. Centers for Disease Control allot very little money for this STD.[7]

Another STD is genital warts (HPV). It is mostly spread by direct contact with an infected person. The more sex partners one has, the greater the risk. There are at least 60 types, 20 of which can infect the genital tract. No wonder the number of cases is increasing in the United States at such a fast pace.

One can get both genital and anal infections. These can be internal as well as external. In fact in one study, eight times as many college women had it on their cervix as in visible places.

In women it can also be on the vulva, on the labia, and inside the vagina. It can be both around the anus and in the rectum. HPV also seems associated with cancer of the genitals, especially the cervix.

In men, the sores can appear on all parts of the penis and the scrotum. If it is inside the urethra, it may cause discharges, bleeding, and a decrease in the flow of urine. On the other hand, there may be no symptoms at all.[8]

164 Can a pregnant mother pass the infection of an STD to her fetus or newborn child?

Sad to say, yes she can. Here are some of the main diseases that she can pass on to her baby:

▶ Syphilis (the baby could be born blind)

▶ Genital herpes, as the child is being born

▶ Gonorrhea

▶ Chlamydia

▶ Genital warts

▶ AIDS, in which the baby will be born to die[9]

Again, what a price to pay for a few risky sex thrills!

165 Other than AIDS, what kinds of STD can be transmitted by oral sex?

Many STDs can be. Some of these are gonorrhea, herpes, genital warts, yeast infection, and syphilis.[10]

166 Can a woman get an STD if the man has one and he touches his penis, then the woman's vagina?

Yes, but that is not too likely. You do need to know, though, that there is some risk.

In all, STD is a nasty business. The smart person will say when tempted to risk exposure: "Thanks, but no thanks."

167 What are the chances of getting an STD?

That depends. There is almost no chance if a person does not engage in intercourse, oral or anal sex, or genital-to-genital and other forms of heavy petting. There is some chance by kissing—especially the deep "tongue-in-cheek" kind—but not much. The chance of getting it from inanimate objects is almost nil.

A half-million new herpes cases in the United States were recorded in 1982. That number has risen sharply each year, and will continue unless a cure is found. One in ten people has herpes II right now.

It is now estimated that two to three percent of all females in the United States have gonorrhea.

168 How can you get tested if you think you might have an STD?

You can't test yourself, that's for sure.

Anyone who even faintly suspects he or she has the signs of an STD should run, not walk, to the nearest doctor or clinic or the public health department for help. The sooner it is treated, the better. And be sure to make a point to ask for an STD test. Just getting a general physical exam is not enough. You have to be clear about what you need.

The sad part of it is that each STD has its own tests or test. No one test could give one a "clean bill of health."[11] So unless you know just which one you have been exposed to, it could be quite a problem.

Almost all cases of gonorrhea and syphilis can be cured now. What the wonder drugs can't do is to restore the body damage that has already been done. But they can prevent any more of it, so quick treatment is of great importance.

If you play with fire long enough, you're sure to get burned. Wouldn't it be better not to put yourself at any kind of risk so you won't have to worry about it? But that is one choice only you can make.

Here's one more bit of news you can feed into that decision. *If you are exposed to an STD, it will raise your risk of getting the HIV (AIDS) virus by at least three times!* And some STDs may speed up the time it takes for the HIV to become a full-blown AIDS infection. Translated, that means you will die sooner than you otherwise would.

Now let's turn our attention to the one that always leads to the painful death of the infected one—AIDS.

PART 14

AIDS: The Killer STD

169 What is HIV and AIDS? Why is it fatal?

AIDS stands for Acquired Immune Deficiency Syndrome. It is one form of sexually transmitted disease. AIDS of itself is not the direct killer. What it does is take away the body's natural ability to fight off infection and disease. It is these latter that actually kill the victim. Thus AIDS pneumonia is just regular pneumonia that the body can not fight off, as normally it would.

The virus that infects a person is called HIV—the Human Immunodeficiency Virus. This highly infectious virus is mostly spread from person to person through some kinds of sexual behavior or the exchange of untested blood.

170 If a person gets AIDS, how long can he or she expect to live?

Once you get AIDS, you will likely die within two years. Few people will live more than three years.[1] And it will be a most miserable kind of death, according to a nurse friend who has attended many victims.

AIDS kills quickly. But there's more bad news. Persons may carry the HIV virus for up to 10 years or more after they are infected. They may not even know they have HIV unless they get a special test.

That means that if you have sex with persons who have done things to put them at risk, they may unwittingly pass it right on to you, too. To be safe, better be careful what you do, and who you associate with! Even one ejaculation could be like a fatal bullet to the heart—but only after months of misery.

171 What are the chances of getting AIDS?

AIDS is spreading like wildfire, not only in the United States, but all over the world. The first case in the United States was found in 1981. Then it took six years to identify the next 50,000 cases. But the next 50,000 took only 18 months. By that time, over 59,000 people had died![2]

In another two years the number of cases jumped to 200,000, and 130,000 had died. As I write, cases have reached well over 250,000 and climbing fast.[3] We should all be deeply concerned and determined to avoid at all costs any risks of getting this deadly menace.

172 How can a person get AIDS?

The good news is that you can't get AIDS from casual contact. You can't get it from a toilet seat. Or a drinking glass. Or a wet towel. Or from a mosquito bite. Or from a kiss. As of now there are no cases on record of it being spread by any such means. In theory, one might get it from one of those passionate "tongue in cheek" deep kisses, but only if there is an exchange of blood from an infected kisser.

In a few cases, HIV has been caught from a professional person, like a dentist or nurse. But these are so rare you need not worry about it. Just see that they wear rubber or plastic gloves when in contact with your blood or sexual fluids.

So it is completely up to you whether you get AIDS. If you avoid any of the behaviors that put you at risk, you won't get it. That's the good news.

The bad news is that if you don't behave yourself, you can put yourself at high risk in a big hurry. As of now there are only four basic ways to get AIDS. Let's list them and discuss them.

1. You can get AIDS *from the exchange of sexual fluids*. This is the main way it is being spread worldwide. Infection is from male to female, and—less often—from female to male. In the United States, it is still more often spread among gay men. But risky male-female cases are catching up fast.[4]
There are two risk factors that are the most common.

   a. One is having many sex partners, especially when they use no protection.[5] In spite of these facts, however, many do not heed the warnings. Those most at risk, use condoms least. One study shows that among all U.S. women aged 15–44:

   ▶ 67% had had more than one partner

   ▶ 41% had had 4 or more partners

   ▶ 23% had had 6 or more, and

   ▶ 8% more than 10.

As for teenagers, 21% had had multiple partners.

And here's the worst part. Only one in five sexually active women said they had used condoms at the last intercourse.[6] That was doubly unwise, since women are more than twice as likely to get AIDS from the male when they have sex than he is to get it from her.[7] That is largely because the ejaculate of an HIV positive male is highly contagious.

Also, a man's semen lies in her inner sex organs for hours after sex. This gives the virus lots of time to be absorbed into her body. It's a dirty trick, women, but that's the sad fact.

Women are most at risk of getting HIV (1) when a man has anal sex with her, (2) when he is in the advanced stages of HIV, and (3) when she is over 45 years of age.

Men are at highest risk when the female is in advanced stages of HIV and when they have unprotected sex during her menstrual period.

Finally, some evidence now suggests that an infected mother may transfer the HIV virus to her child through breast feeding.[8]

b. The other high risk behavior is being involved with penile-anal sex.[9] The reason seems clear. The anus is not made for sexual intercourse. It is made for quite a different purpose. That means that in anal sex the tender membranes will likely be scraped or ruptured. This allows the HIV virus to enter the body. Often there will be bleeding, so that the virus can get right into the person's bloodstream. Infection can be instant.

2. The second way you can get AIDS is by *the exchange of infected blood*. This is most likely to happen when several persons shoot drugs or steroids with the same needle. If the needle enters the bloodstream of a person with HIV, every person who then uses the needle will be exposed.

It is one of the best reasons I know to stay completely away from drugs. I hope none of you ever do it. Or if you are already doing it, I hope you will vow to stop it this very minute.

In rare cases, one can get AIDS through tiny microscopic cuts or breaks anywhere on the skin.[10]

3. You can get AIDS *from oral sex*. Until recently, we didn't think that was possible, since human saliva is not a good

170

carrier of the virus. However, at least two clinical cases have now been reported. I suspect that exposure happens when a mouth that is receiving the infected semen has a bleeding gum or cold sore. Or the person may have bit their lip or tongue or cheek. That allows the virus a way into the bloodstream.

4. Finally, *an infected mother can give her unborn baby AIDS*. The baby will be born to die. And all because the mother put herself at risk for getting AIDS through sex or drugs.

173 What are the chances of getting AIDS from French kissing?

Almost nil. It could only happen if the tongue was bleeding and the mouth was also. It would be an exchange of infected blood. There is no recorded case of it being spread that way as of this writing.

174 What's the best method of birth control to prevent AIDS?

As we have said, the condom is the only one to give any protection at all. Yet few people use them.

In the high risk areas of San Francisco, fewer than one in 10 persons having male/female intercourse say they always use condoms.[11]

Why do so few people at risk use the only method that gives any protection? Here are some of the reasons they give researchers:

▶ Too embarrassed to buy them

▶ Reduced sensations for the male

▶ Might send the message that you have AIDS

▶ Might imply that you think your partner has AIDS[12]

For these reasons they risk their very lives? It's hard to believe, isn't it? And we humans are supposed to be the most intelligent species on earth!

175 You said that you and most other scientists think AIDS will spread most rapidly in the adolescent population in the 1990s. Why is that?

In less than three years—1986 to 1988—AIDS moved up from the seventh to the sixth leading cause of death among those who are 15-24 years of age.[13] And the rates are still climbing fast.

During the 1980s, the number of women aged 15-19 years old who had had sex moved from 47 to 53 percent. The men moved from 66 to 76 percent[14]—from two-thirds to three-fourths. Quite a jump.

In New York City, 60 to 70 percent of the teen runaways had sex in the previous three months. Yet 27 percent of the men and 47 percent of the women said they never used a condom.[15]

And what about junior high youth? One study centered on 7th and 8th graders. Compared to their nonactive peers, those who were sexually active differed in several ways:

▶ They tended to have less knowledge about AIDS.

▶ They were less fearful that they would get it.

▶ They showed less tolerance of people with AIDS.

▶ They were more likely to engage in risky behavior.[16]

So they worry less and gamble more. No wonder AIDS is creeping into our junior high and middle school population.

176 **What can we do to try to stop this epidemic of risky teen sex activity? Do we just have to let it run its course and hope for the best?**

There's much we can do—and are doing.

For one thing, awareness of the risks is beginning to sink in with those who insist on having sex. For women and urban males, use of condoms at first intercourse doubled from 1982 to 1988. And teen men who had AIDS education had fewer partners and greater condom use than those who did not.[17]

But young people these days don't respond much to being preached at or moralized to. What they do respond to are facts, backed up by responsible research.

A national survey was conducted in 1992. It showed that instruction in the skills one needs to resist sexual intercourse had a stronger influence on reducing sex activity than did instruction about AIDS and birth control.[18]

In another study, researchers found that the more teens knew about HIV, the more they changed their behavior.

▶ 6% stopped having sex due to fear of AIDS

▶ 45% were having sex less than before they knew

▶ 58% were having fewer partners

▶ 58% were using condoms more often than before[19]

One interesting fact. Females are more likely to get AIDS from intercourse. Yet it is the males who are more anxious about getting AIDS. I, too, have found that good facts about abstinence get good results. At one school, a surprising 66 percent of the 800 students moved toward abstinence after I spoke.[20]

177 **If I shared a needle over a year ago, should I be worried?**

Maybe you should be. The HIV virus may linger in your body for many years before you finally get AIDS. To be on the safe side, I would get tested for HIV very soon.

178 If you were tested for AIDS seven years ago after a blood transfusion, could you still have AIDS?

No, not unless you have exposed yourself to the HIV in the time since then. After about 1986, all blood given in transfusions by law has to be tested for the HIV virus.

179 Where can you get tested for AIDS?

It takes two tests—one now, and one six months or so from now. If both test results are negative and you have had no risk behavior in between, then you are not infected.

To get the test, call your local public health agency or a physician or AIDS counselor. They will keep it confidential if you make that request. If none of these suggestions are good in your case, then call this toll-free number and ask for help: 1-800-342-AIDS.

PART 15

Is Living-In Flunking Out?

180 What do you think about living together before you are married. Is it a good or a bad idea?

I doubt that it's important to you what *I* think about it. It's more important what *you* think about it. We do know some valid facts about this practice that should be shared.

For one thing, all of the negative aspects of sex before marriage apply to this situation. Live-ins are also sleep-ins. Out of hundreds of live-in couples studied by scientists, only one was found who said they were not having sex. So the guilt, the fear of getting pregnant, of getting caught, of getting STDs, and of being robbed of that highly important "sexual cement"—all these would apply as well with the live-ins.

Living together carries the risks of flunking the test of time, of having sexual salivation, and of having a less happy marriage. In most cases it involves being dishonest by deceiving parents and family as well as friends and others about whom one cares. Further, it is considered to be a serious sin in the eyes of all the major religions, at least as of now.

Apart from all that, living-in is just not working out. Live-ins are less likely to marry. If they do marry, they're less likely to have a good marriage. That comes as a great shock to most people. It cuts across common sense. After all, how can one better prove a relationship than by being together day by day and in all kinds of situations?

Even scientists are for the most part surprised. We have known for years, for instance, that the longer the courtship and the engagement, the better the chance of a good marriage. So would it not follow that living-in would be the best way of all to get to know the other well?

In this case, common sense is once again proved wrong. We will point out some of the reasons why in a moment. But first, let's see how the living-in patterns have changed in the past decade or two. These facts may prove of help to those who consider doing it.

First, let us review a summary of typical traits of unwed U.S. live-in couples and their relationships back in 1984. These traits were compiled from the best research findings as of that date. They are discussed in the questions. Some of the research was carried out just as the live-in pattern began to blossom. Studies since have revealed very few major changes in those particular results.

As you study the following 1984 chart, watch for several things. Look for signs that live-ins are mature or not mature. For their part, they see maturity as the main requirement for living-in. Are they or aren't they being mature?

Look also for signs that one partner is using the other. If so, who is using whom? How so? Who's coming out on the short end of the deal?

Many of the findings in early studies have not been re-tested in recent research. These items will be retained in their former form. Where they have changed, that will be noted in this profile. The regular print means items were not changed by more recent findings. Hence they may or may not still be valid for college live-ins. Confirmed in bold print indicates that late studies do affirm the former findings.

When you've studied the chart, I'll have some comments about it in the context of questions youth have asked. Then we can compare those results with the new findings from the very recent research.

Profile of Unwed U.S. Live-In Couples and Their Relationships

Typical Live-In Couples   ### Typical Live-In Males

A. *General Characteristics*

- Live in large cities and/or attend college.
- Represent fewer than 3% of all couples living together, but this unmarried portion has been growing dramatically. (**Confirmed**)
- Have had less happy adolescence than going-together couples.
- See themselves as independent, outgoing, aggressive personalities.
- See maturity as the prime requirement for living-in.
- Have low personal guilt; low perception of social disapproval.

- Less likely to come from unstable home backgrounds than their partner.
- More likely to physically abuse their partner than married males.

B. *Marriage Prospects*

- Believe in marriage in theory but have low level of commitment to it with current partner. (**Confirmed**)
- Will likely be poor marriage risk. (**Confirmed**)
- Differ on the question of marriage, whereas going-together couples both

- See living-in as a personal convenience rather than an emotional involvement. (**Confirmed**)
- Have little or no intent to marry the woman. (**Confirmed**)
- Deceive partner; if pressed to make a commitment to marry, put off partner with excuses

Typical Live-In Females	Typical Relationships
• Rated their parents' marriage as "unhappy" twice as often as did men.	• Relatively new lifestyle for unmarried U.S. middle-class youth.
• About two-thirds come from divorced or unhappy homes.	• "Drifted into" rather than a well-thought-out decision.
• Come from homes with divorced parents 2-3 times as often as men.	• Encounter few problems arising from outside community, school, administrations, etc.; but
• 85 out of 86 say they think it is not wrong to live-in before marriage.	• Experience many conflicts, problems, guilts, and embarrassments.
• Experience more physical abuse than wives get from husbands.	
• Claim to feel little or no guilt either before or after; yet	
• Mention negative public opinion most often as the disadvantage of living-in.	

• List desire for marriage and security as first choice of reasons for living-in.	• An arrangement for convenience, not for keeps.
• As undergrads, do not consider themselves married in any sense of the word.	• Stay together a short time as live-ins (mean–9.6 months). (**Confirmed**; now 1.3 years)
• If women get their way, marriage rates will remain the same. (**Confirmed**)	• Share far fewer of the key feelings known to be essential in a good marriage compared to

Typical Live-In Couples

agree they're headed for marriage. (**Confirmed**)

Typical Live-In Males

like "wait until I get a job" or "after we graduate" or "I don't want to be tied down just yet."
• If men get their way, marriage rates will go down. (**Confirmed**)
• See living-in as substitute, not prelude to marriage. (**Confirmed**)

C. Parental Attitudes

• 10% of their parents actually approve.
• 66% of their parents disapprove; some parents are neutral.
• Are unwilling or afraid to inform parents; yet
• Continue to accept parental favors.

• 50% keep living-in a secret from parents.
• Depend less on parents for protection and approval than women.

D. Financial Aspects

• Have relatively low incomes and high unemployment. (**Confirmed**)
• Keep own funds separate. (**Confirmed**)
• Often still accept parents' support and favors; although

• Seldom provide full financial support to partner. (**Confirmed**)
• 19% work full time and do not attend school.
• 11% both work and attend school.

Typical Live-In Females

- More likely to experience marriage failure if she pressures male into marriage. (**Confirmed**)
- View a commitment to marry as an important part of the arrangement, particularly for those with unhappy adolescence and high need for the partner.

Typical Relationships

going-together couples:
  —less shared need for each other
  —less respect for the other
  —fewer feelings of being happy
  —less mutual involvement
  —less commitment to marriage. (**Confirmed**)
- Have a poorer chance of having a good marriage than do going-together couples. (**Confirmed**)

- 65–75% keep it a secret from their parents.
- Depends more on parents and fears their rejection more than males. (**Confirmed**)
- Keeps some clothes, etc., in dorm/sorority room or apartment with other women, partly as a front to deceive parents.

- Parents seen as a "major problem area" since they seldom approve.

- Far more likely to quit school and work full time.
- 30% work full time and do not attend school.
- 15% both work and attend school.

- Half again as many of the women quit school to work full time.
- Seldom totally pool resources.
- Fight most often about finances—just like spouses do.

Typical Live-In Couples	**Typical Live-In Males**
• Fewer couples receive parental support than in years past (a drop from 33% to 14% in only five years).	

E. Sex Patterns

• 100% of both sexes have had previous sex experience. (**Confirmed**)	• List access to regular sexual gratification as main reason for living-in. • Are increasingly becoming "mattress hoppers"—going from one partner to another with little or no emotional commitment to any. (**Confirmed**)

F. Emotional Involvement

• Do not consider their relationship as a "trial marriage." • Do not view love as a necessary element for cohabiting.	• Lack feelings of respect and need for their partner. • Often take live-in relationship lightly, with little or no emotional involvement.

Typical Live-In Females	**Typical Relationships**
• Interested only secondarily in sex gratification. • All use some contraceptive, usually the pill. • Likely to feel she's "being used" or exploited. • Worry that male sometimes sleeps around, yet feels helpless to stop it.	• Fight frequently because man is also sleeping with other women (listed as second highest cause). • Tend to have many sexual problems—differing levels of sex interest, lack of orgasm, fear of pregnancy, etc.
• More likely to get serious and emotionally involved with partner. • More likely to experience jealousy. • May feel trapped.	• Viewed more as an indulgence in intimacy while "going steady" than as a trial marriage. • Only 9% already engaged to marry. • Frequently become overinvolved and can't just walk out like they'd thought they could.

181 **Is living together unwed all that new? Haven't some people always been doing it?**

There have always been some who lived-in unwed. Some states have laws about it and refer to it as "common law marriages." That is, if a couple live together for a certain span of time and present themselves to the public as being married, they can then be called legally married.

In the small Idaho town of Emmett where I grew up, a neighbor man did just that. His wife had died some years before. All of a sudden he brought home a woman to live with him. But the poor woman paid a tragic price, and so did he. How the gossip tongues did wag! None of the neighbors were even civil, much less friendly to her, and they were pretty cool to him as well. I've often thought how much better it would have been all around if they had just gotten married. Why put themselves through such an awful ordeal? It just didn't make sense. And it still doesn't.

The new thing in living-in now is *who* is doing it. Starting in the late 1960s when Vietnam was such a source of unrest among the young, more and more college students took up the practice. Most of them were from middle-class families. That was new. Living together is far more common at large city universities in the Northeast and the Far West than anywhere else. It is least practiced in the South.

The type of person involved is also of great interest. It should come as no surprise that the males doing it are fairly average types. The amount of premarital sex among males has not changed all that much. Their dads and granddads were just about as sexually active when they were young as this generation of males is. But now males are doing it much more often and at much younger ages.

The big shift has come with the females. Far more of them have begun to be sexually active in the past 30 years than ever before. By and large, women going for the live-in idea are not those from stable, happy, two-parent homes. Two out of every three of them came from broken or unhappy homes, about three times as many as the men. And twice as many of the women thought their parents' marriage was "unhappy" as did the men.

182 Why are so many more couples living together without being married these days?

There are many reasons. One is that premarital sex has become more common. Another is that young people are alarmed at the number of divorces and poor marriages they see all around them. Many have lived through a divorce in their own family. They do not want to make the same mistakes themselves. They think that if they live together they can avoid those mistakes. At least that's the theory, and this younger generation has swallowed it—hook, line, and waterbed.

Sadly enough, this theory seems to have more holes in it than a slice of Swiss cheese. For one thing, most college couples who are living-in just drift into it. It is not a reasoned, well-planned decision such as, "We'll do this to curb the high rates of poor marriage." Or "We'll try this out as a test to see if we'd have a good marriage." They do not talk it over at length and decide to do it on the merits of the case. Instead, most couples first become involved in sex. Then they have sex in her room, after which the guy will dress and go home. In time he does not want to leave, so he doesn't. He just stays the night. Finally they just move in with each other.

Another cause for so much living-in is simply that women are letting it happen. This is not sexism, it is just a fact of life. There have always been plenty of men who were ready to have sex with a woman at the drop of an eyelash. It is still true that the woman more often than not is the one who decides whether there will be sex in a relationship and on what terms. As long as she's willing to give sex without any commitment on his part, she will find lots of men who will be more than willing to oblige. Men in a living-in situation have it pretty soft. They get all of the privileges of being wed—regular sex, a housekeeper, etc.—without any of the tough responsibilities. The rather rare exception is where he may have to pay her "palimony."

In my view, one basic reason why many women have decided to live-in is their own poor home experience. What does that suggest? To me it seems clear that these women have been deprived of good, solid male relationships in their homes. They miss out on having a healthy male role model.

Many of these women grew up in one-parent homes. Since mothers get custody of the children in almost every divorce, the girls were robbed of a close day-to-day relation with a father. By living-in, in my view, they are trying to make up for their loss.

Will they succeed in filling that need? Sad to say, most of them likely will not. Most of their live-in partners have little or no intention of getting serious. So when the break comes, as it usually does, such a woman may well be emotionally worse off than she was before. She trusted a man and he let her down. Each new partner she gets and then loses will just further deepen her problem. It will leave her even more deprived, I fear. She is looking in the wrong places to satisfy her basic need. She will, alas, likely be destined to disappointment.

183 Is living together really trial marriage?

For the most part it certainly is not. Many use that as the excuse to justify their actions. But they will admit to researchers that in no sense do they think of it as a trial marriage. I call this, then, the "Trial Marriage Myth." As we have seen, most of the males see living-in as an alternative to, and not a preparation for, marriage. If the subject of marriage comes up, they either lie or hedge. They make excuses. But in fact, they may have no intention at all of ever marrying their partner. And, by the way, is he being mature??

Now in most live-in relationships, the man won't tell that to the woman. It is still true that very few women in the United States will have sex with a man unless they feel real love in the relationship. A man may admit to a researcher, who is sworn to secrecy, that he won't marry his partner, but if he told *her* the truth, he'd likely lose his warm bed.

When I made that statement on an early morning radio call-in show some time back, the interviewer in Miami let out a big, lusty guffaw. "What's so funny?" I asked. "Oh, I can just see dozens of young men all over town getting kicked out of bed right now," he laughed. Happy landings, fellows!

Some day soon I think many of the women who are now living-in are going to wise up. When I was young there was an old saying among the guys. "Why buy the cow if you can get the milk free?" Aside from the put-down comparison with a bovine, women, what do you say to that one? How long are you going to let the men get by with that?

For most men it's an arrangement for convenience, not for keeps. Back in 1984, the average college live-in relation lasted only about 8 to 9½ months, which is roughly the length of a school year. The next school year a man will find another sex partner. No wonder one girl complained to a researcher, "Sometimes I get the feeling I'm being used."

More recently, since the practice of cohabiting has more and more moved off campus, the average length of a live-in is now 1.3 years. That's still a pretty brief span of time.

But what if a woman does talk her live-in partner into marrying her? What are the chances of their making a go of it? Not good, says the research—both then and now. When "going-together" couples were compared to "living-togethers," the going-togethers came out way ahead. They were more likely to marry than the live-ins. And if they did marry, they had much better marriages. The going-togethers had far more of those elements we've known for a long time are the signs of a good marriage. So their chances of good marriages were far better than those of the live-in couples. Maybe the time has come to sound retreat from the live-in hang-up.

184 Why isn't living together the best way to go? There are no ties. If it doesn't work out you can just walk away. It would save you the tragedy of divorce and all that legal hassle.

Many couples have found that getting out of a live-in is not as simple as they had thought. They can't just "shake and break." They had thought both of them would be able to say, "Well, so long. It was nice knowing you." Instead one of them said, "Oh, no! Please, please don't leave me. I'll just die if you do." When two people share a day-and-night relationship as intimate as living together, one or the other of them runs a great risk of getting serious. This happens to the woman far more than to the man. She is more likely to relate sex to love. After all, in the sex act her body is being penetrated. She is being exposed to the possibility of having a baby, with all the life burdens and duties it would involve. And what if she does get pregnant? He can—and often does—just split. Legally, there is little or nothing she can do about it. He is not bound unless he wants to be. It's all up to him. She's completely at his mercy. And he at hers.

I recall one case where a couple lived together for years. They saved and bought a home and car and nice furniture. She had two children by him. He kept saying he'd marry her some day, but he never did. Then one day he was killed in an auto crash. She was left with nothing. The home and car—even the man's life insurance—went to his parents and his brothers. She and the children had no legal claim at all, even to what she had worked so hard to help get.

188

Had they been married, she and her children would have had it all. Instead they got zilch.

Live-ins share another problem with couples who are married. We're now seeing just about as many broken hearts from live-in breakups as we used to see from broken engagements or marriages. A broken heart hurts just as much from a live-in breakup as from any other kind. And if one's parents have not approved of the situation, one of the most important sources of solace and sympathy may be gone. Their attitude may be: "You made your bed. Now lie in it." There is often no place to turn for understanding and help.

There's yet another problem. When a live-in couple breaks up, what about the property settlement? This problem is worse with live-ins than in a divorce. Why? No community property laws apply here. Both have chipped in to buy things. So who gets what? In one case I knew, the guy waited for a night when his partner wasn't home. Then he just drove up with a truck, loaded in everything of value and left. She couldn't even go to the police. She had no legal claim or proof of ownership. She was just out.

But more often there is a real clash over what belongs to whom. There are bitter words and hard feelings that last for years, just as in a divorce.

Finally, even if there is no breakup, there can be a lot of heartaches. Since there are no vows and usually no contract, both parties may feel free to have other intimate relations. That can cause a lot of misery for the one who cares the most for their live-in partner. If you really care for someone whom you know is also sleeping around with others, your heart bleeds a lot. There is jealousy. There is a feeling of helplessness. There will likely be harsh words and even fights. Since some men take their live-in relationships quite casually, once again it is the woman who most often gets hurt. The male "mattress hoppers" can leave a tragic trail of broken hearts and human misery in their wake. So will women if they do the same thing.

185 Won't living together be a good test of our sex life before marriage?

Your question makes a big assumption—that couples who live together will marry. Many will not, as we have seen—although this seems to be changing some now.

Even so, living together may not be a good test of your sex life at all. If you have sex you are almost certain to feel guilt, fear, and loss of self-regard. It's a no-no and you know it. Hence these guilts and fears and anxieties will keep you from having full satisfaction with your sex life. But if you wait for sex until you marry, this should not happen. There will then be no need to feel guilt or fear.

Some people may wrongly reason: "If our sex life is not good before we marry, it won't be good after." That may not be true at all. A girl who is too uptight while she is single to enjoy sex may be fully relaxed and a fine sex partner after she's a wife.

On the other hand, sex before marriage may be more exciting than it will be after. Before marriage it is forbidden fruit. You may enjoy it more, simply because you think you're getting away with something you're not supposed to do. (We get a lot of unwed pregnancies that way!) After marriage, the forbidden factor is gone. Your sex life may be more dull, and hence a disappointment.

Either way, sex before marriage is not a true test of what it will be like afterward.

Studies show that live-ins in fact have pretty much the same problems and hang-ups with sex as married couples. They complain about lack of orgasm. Their levels of interest in sex are often not the same. And even more than married couples, they have a fear of pregnancy (in spite of their use of birth control).

And then there's the problem of cheating, which is more likely to happen with live-ins. One woman said sadly: "I know he's having sex with other women, but there's not a thing I can do about it. If we were married I wouldn't let him get by with it."

Of course there are other dangers in this besides her mental anguish. Her partner could get another woman pregnant. Or the guy just might bring home some STD—or even AIDS. That could be a lifelong disaster for her if it happened to be herpes II or some other strain of STD for which there is no known cure.

186 Isn't it cheaper to live together than apart?

In some ways, yes. Housing, furnishings, and utility costs can be shared. But strange as it may seem, few of the live-ins pool their finances. Most keep their own funds quite separate from their partner's. One reason may be that many still accept money from home, but wish to deceive their parents. A joint checking account might well blow their cover. The male seldom gives full financial support. And when they break up, as most of them do, there may be that big hassle over what belongs to whom.

One more point to note here is that women who are in college seem to be doing most of the giving in the live-in arrangement. They are far more likely to quit school and work full time. Half again as many women as men do so. And more women than men work and go to school at the same time. One might ask: Who's getting the raw end of that deal?

In times past, a girl used to give sex in exchange for love, a home, and a meal ticket. In the live-in pattern, she gives (and gets) sex *and* shells out most of the dollars as well. Let's play back that girl's complaint: "Sometimes I get the feeling I'm being used." Now, I wonder why?

We must not leave the impression that all men who live-in use their partners. I'm sure many take great care to be fair. Nor are all the women without blame in this regard. Some of them use the men more than they themselves are used. However, research does suggest that women are the victims much more often than they are the offenders.

191

Wanted: a New Direction for Women's Liberation

In the name of women's liberation, I'm afraid that many women have jumped out of the frying pan right into the fire. They have rebelled—and rightly so—against the double standard in sex. They resent the fact that many non-virgin grooms expect their brides to be virgins. And who can blame them? Why shouldn't the male be a virgin, too?

Yet by plunging into easy sex, as some women have done, they have just opened themselves up to new ways of being used. In the name of being more free, they have accepted a new kind of slavery. By being willing to share sex without love or commitment, they have set themselves up for an entirely new way of being used by men. Instead of insisting that men come up to their own high standards, women have lowered theirs to the level of the men.

A great opportunity has been missed. Since more and more of us men rebel at the double standard, too, women are now in a position to shape the change. Why can't the sexual revolution be *a moral step up on the part of men?* Why must it instead be a step down by women? If women would lead the way, it could be done. A lot of us men would support them to the hilt.

187 **Why do so many parents blow their cool if their kids live together before marriage?**

You are so right. Most moms and dads don't like the idea one bit. In 1984, only 10 percent of the parents of live-ins gave it their blessing. I doubt if that has changed much. And I suspect that most of those who do approve are the parents of the males.

That's one reason why so many more women do not tell their folks what is going on. One girl told a researcher, "If my dad knew what I was doing he'd drag me home from college by the hair of my head."

Are parents just old-fashioned, out of date, and not with it? Some certainly are, but their concern may well run deeper than tradition. For one thing, they probably love their kids. If they do, they don't want them to get hurt. So if they sense that their loved ones are being used or doing something that they will come to regret, parents will try to shield them from harm if possible. That's just the way parental love works.

Also, many parents still support their children when they are in college. They may deeply resent the fact that their money may go to support a relationship they feel is not good. This may be why fewer and fewer parents are giving full support to their live-in offspring—a drop from 33 percent to 14 percent in only six years.

Many parents are wary of the so-called "new morality." Their suspicions seem justified. Living-in is a scheme that has not yet been proven successful. Couples who go together have been shown to be on much safer turf than those who live together.

Parents also oppose living-in for the same reasons they are against premarital sex. They fear a case of STDs or AIDS, a pregnancy, abortion, or a shotgun wedding—the whole bit. But alas, the loving concern of parents may fall on deaf ears. Most couples who live together see moms and dads as a big pain.

The moral problem of honesty must also be raised here. Many live-ins, especially women, go to great lengths to deceive their folks. They keep some clothes and other things in their dorm room or apartment where their parents are led to believe they are staying. In case mom or dad drop by without notice, it all looks like it's on the up and up. Their roomie is in on the lie. She says very innocently, "Oh, I think she's over at the library. I'll go get her." She runs down the hall and calls, "You'd better get your tail over here fast! Your mom and dad just breezed in."

Are the brief pleasures of living-in worth that kind of dishonesty with those who love you? And what if your parents find out anyway, as well they might? These questions need to be carefully thought through.

Another moral issue has to do with money. Is it cheating to keep getting money from your parents under false pretense? Is it fair to take money you know they would withhold if they knew what you were doing with it? Is that being mature?

These are decisions only a person who is living-in can make. But in all fairness the issues ought to be raised.

One further question might be asked. Even if you do save a few dollars by living together, what is the cost to your integrity? To your long-range values? What of the risk that you won't marry, or be less happy if you do? Is it being mature to deceive one you claim to care about? I think not.

188 **What do you think about living together after courtship but before marriage? For example, two couples I know went steady for several years. Then they decided to live together to make sure they could get along with each other. They each got married and are still happily married.**

That is the only way that living together *may* serve to help, not hinder, good marriages. In such cases the living together is a final stage of engagement. Both parties have pretty well decided that their relationship is for keeps. *They have a commitment.* They just want a kind of "final exam" before they take their public vows. Quite apart from the moral issues or sin involved, such a plan may in some cases have some good results.

In the United States it has never been the case that the "piece of paper" was what made a couple married. Their mutual pledge to each other is the real key. The marriage certificate is just the evidence which states that their vows have been accepted as legal by society. It's a social "stamp of approval."

But if they are that sure of their relationship, the act of living together is really not likely to be of much added value. Why put themselves through the hassle? Why risk the wrath of parents, friends, and others who care? Why do what many will condemn as sinful and a violation of the will of God? Why expose yourself and the person you care about to feelings of guilt and fear? Why risk a forced marriage through pregnancy? Why not just give your relationship more time if you still have doubts, and then just get married and avoid all the ruckus? That would seem the sounder way to go.

This raises the question of maturity. Is it being mature to use another person for one's own selfish ends? Is it being mature to allow one's self to be used by another? Is it being mature to lie and deceive those who love and care for you? Is it mature to have sex with other people and then come back and expect to shack up with your live-in partner?

All in all, it would seem that the live-ins fail their own test. They say that maturity is the prime requirement for doing it. Yet the evidence seems to show that they are by no means showing the traits that are usually thought to be evidence of mature, grown-up behavior.

Let us now turn our attention to what is new on the living-in front.

189 Much of the research cited is pretty old. Does it really apply to us any more?

Let's have a look at some facts. The following list shows the results of the very latest research that we could find. It comes from some of the most reliable sources in this field of science. Most of it was published within just four years of this writing.*

*For the list of sources used in the more recent research, see Appendix 3.

As compared to those who don't cohabit, those who do:

a. Have had more sexual experiences, and had sex at younger ages.

b. Will have more sexual partners, making them more likely to contract sexually transmitted diseases (STDs) like AIDS, and to get pregnant.

c. Are less likely to hold traditional family values.

d. Are more likely to break up than couples who just go together, which tends to weaken their faith in marriage itself.

e. Have more discord when they do break up.

f. Tend to date much more often as college students, and to have sexual coitus with their dates.

g. Are more likely to approve of sex before marriage and of living-in—since frequency of both has increased since 1984.

h. Tend to be more nonconformist and nontraditional.

i. Show greater use of drugs—cocaine, marijuana, etc.—as well as amphetamines. Alcohol is the drug of choice.

j. Tend to be "risk takers" and are poorer marriage risks, especially those who have lived-in a number of times before they marry.

k. Tend to have lower education.

l. Choose abortion as the most likely course if pregnancy occurs.

m. Tend to be further along in their development—are on a "faster track." But show some signs of not being very mature, such as not taking full responsibility for their actions.

n. Are less committed to each other; it's a "looser bond."

o. Are less likely to choose a partner of the same age or religion.

p. Are more unstable in their employment and personal lives.

q. Are less interested in having and rearing children.

r. Have fewer things in common in their relationship and are less alike in their thinking and attitudes.

Other general facts about cohabitors follow:

a. The trend toward unwed living-in has been led by the least well-educated part of our population.

b. They favor equality of men and women and approve of single parenthood.

c. Most cohabs end within two years, but more—50 to 60 percent—of these now do end in marriage.

d. Cohabitors tend to choose partners with about the same amount of education.

e. Our society still values monogamy, but as cohabiting gets more frequent, it tends to undermine the idea of just one relationship for keeps.

f. Cohabitors are more similar to singles than to marrieds. It is mainly an alternative to being single.

g. Live-in men are much less likely to marry than the women. By age 23.5, 30 percent of women have exited single life through marriage, but fewer than half as many (14 percent) of the men had done so.

h. Males are still more likely to cohabit than women—two-thirds of the men compared to one-half of the women in one study.

i. In spite of their claims of being liberated from tradition, cohabitors still exhibit some sexism. If they have children, they tend to teach male and female roles, steer males more into sports and females into more nurturant behavior.

j. If parents have had their marriage fail, their children are more likely to cohabit unmarried.

k. Young adults who live at home are less likely to cohabit.

l. Youth with strong religious beliefs are less likely to cohabit.

m. It's not "trial marriage" and not good training for marriage.

n. They plan to marry and have children "some day" but are in no rush to do so.

o. When mothers approve of living-in, their live-in children are less likely to marry; but

p. When mothers do not approve, the children are less likely to cohabit.

q. Mothers have more influence over whether their daughters cohabit than they do over their sons' choices. This difference is partly because young women are more subject to sanctions when they defy parental wishes or depart from "accepted" behavior.

r. Marriage to the live-in partner is more likely to happen if the woman was highly religious in her adolescence.

s. If the couple use illegal drugs, their live-in arrangement is more likely to be dissolved without marriage.

190 **What effect will living-in unwed have on my marriage?**

It will likely have very real effects, most of which tend to be negative. A host of recent studies—at least nine—confirm that those who cohabit before they marry are more likely to:

▶ Reduce their chances of getting married.

▶ Have a more unstable marriage.

▶ Have the marriage end in divorce or separation—including a 46 percent greater chance of former live-ins having their marriage fail.

▶ Will run a greater risk of having their marriage break up, particularly for women cohabitors who marry young.

▶ Experience an even higher rate of marital failure if they are serial cohabitors.

▶ Be able to use a history of live-in breakups as a predictor of breakups after marriage.

▶ Reduce the risks of breakup—about 70 percent for men and 64 percent for women—with the birth of the first child.

▶ Use drugs after they marry, the most common being alcohol, followed by marijuana.

191 **If a couple like each other a lot, why isn't it a good idea to test your relationship by living together first?**

It is too bad that this young person did not have the chance to study all of the information just listed above. If she or he had, this question might not have been asked.

In spite of all these negative factors, the practice of cohabitating is growing by leaps and bounds. Perhaps people just hear what they want to hear. The research facts just roll off them like water off a duck's back. There is still widespread faith in the old idea that cohabitating before marriage is a good test of marital happiness and success.

But all scientists can do is to provide the facts. It is up to each person to decide whether to heed those facts. As the folklore of old puts it: You can lead a horse to water, but you can't make it drink.

The preceding summaries may well be the most complete profile of cohabitation to be found in any one place as of now. It is included here so the reader can make an informed judgment as to whether it is wise to be involved in this kind of practice.

192 I like my boyfriend very much, but now he is trying to push me into living together and having sex. What should I do?

No matter how fond you are of him, no one has a right to push you into doing what you don't wish to do. It is your life and your body. What you do when you are with him is up to you, not up to him, your peers, or anyone else. You must be your own person.

Why not sit down and have a long talk about it? Try to talk sense. Share with him those eleven known facts. Point out that scientists have found that premarital sex will likely decrease your chances of marrying each other. Mention that you'll be less likely to have a happy and lasting marriage. Chances are he has not heard these facts. You may even insist that he read this book. Or better yet, you could read it together and then discuss it. That may well help change his mind and solve your problem.

Then talk about the typical profile of U.S. live-ins. Point out that in most cases it is not working out. It is seldom trial marriage.

Ask him if he'd rather have sex now and take all those risks. Note that the chances are that it would rob both of you of much of your married happiness.

Then ask yourself: If he really loved me, would he want to expose me to the risk of an unwed pregnancy? Would he want me to get all that flack from friends and parents that I would get by living with him? If he really loved me, would he want to hurt me?

Most likely he will listen to reason. But stand your ground. Don't be pressured. If he still insists on being pushy, tell him to shove off. He may have more interest in sex than in you. If so, good riddance.

193 Does "living together" always mean having sex? Or can it be a period of time to see how it works with each other without sex?

It can be, but it won't be. It is, of course, quite possible for two to live-in and not be into sex. But do they?

As a rule, no. They don't refrain from sex. In the dozens of couples questioned in four major studies, only one pair said they were not having sex. If we assume these two were telling the truth, it's still safe to say that live-ins are having sex. The chances are well over 100 to one.

194 Do you think living-in is just a passing fad, or will it become the new pattern of courtship in our society?

It's hard to say. But there is now some evidence that the pendulum has swung to its limit and is now on the way back. Here are some of the clues that suggest this trend.

1. Reports of the 1980 census showed a huge increase in the number of persons living together but not married. There had been about a 10-fold increase in the last 10 years. However, the number of persons in the *younger* age brackets showed a much *slower* increase than what

it had been the previous year. That suggests that the younger ages may have begun to rethink the practice.

2. Many counselors and authors report that younger sisters are being warned not to live with guys. Older sisters who did so and got burned are passing the word: "This ain't the way to go." It seems that little sister is starting to get the picture.

3. My own research has shown the same shift in student thinking. In the past 30 years the attitudes of my college students have gone full circle. In the early 1960s, almost all students rejected premarital sex. Only a few thought it was wise to do it. Ten years later, in the Vietnam era, the trend was just reversed. Most thought it wise, few thought it not wise. Now once again they reject premarital sex by a rather large margin. Views on living-in have tended to follow the same trend.

All this seems to suggest that a more thoughtful, long-term view of sexuality is in the works and may in fact prevail. It does seem that a return to more stable relationships may well be in the wind. It bears watching.

PART 16

The Guilt Trip Trauma

195 **In *Sex, Love, or Infatuation,* you state that guilts and fears that come when one has premarital sex will carry over and help ruin one's sex life after marriage. I disagree. I don't think young people these days feel that it's wrong, especially if they really care about each other.**

That is the way many *think,* but is that the way they really *feel* deep down inside? What may seem right at the time may come back to haunt us a few years down the pike. Most counselors and pastors know that the guilt can be both deep and lasting. Take for example this sad letter that I received from a young woman:

> Dear Prof. Short:
>   Several years ago I heard you speak at a nearby high school. I skipped school that day to hear you talk and I ended up learning two things: (1) You get in trouble when you cut classes (even to go to another school!) and (2) Premarital sex isn't worth the consequences.
>   Well, somewhere along the way I forgot about those lessons. And it seems that one of them had a bigger impact on my life than I ever dreamed of.

About two and one-half years after I first heard you speak, Mr. Right came along, and unlike the fairytales, my *dreamboy* lover turned out to be a *nightmare*.

I'm 20 now, and the fact that someone knows me inside and out still hurts after two whole years. And somehow I get the feeling it will never go away.

This brings me to my reason for writing to you. Since my senior year in high school (when I first heard you), you came to my campus to speak. The one thing I needed from you was some kind of advice for those who are past the point of no return.

I will be attending your talk at the Minneapolis Lutheran Youth Congress during the last week in December. Could you please give a few words of encouragement to those of us (maybe it's just me) who had to learn the hard way that sex before marriage isn't smart? And that if you have to have sex with someone just to keep them, they aren't worth keeping?

I have run into a lot of jerks who can't understand why a girl who isn't a virgin doesn't sleep around anymore, and it makes me feel kind of freakish.

Your advice at the Congress would be much appreciated, even if just a few words.

> Thanks a bunch,
> Julie (*not her real name*)

My heart bleeds for Julie and the many others like her.

During my workshop at a National Christian Youth Congress a girl stood up and said to those 700 students: "Hey! Listen to what this guy is saying to you. He is absolutely right. I had to learn the hard way."

She went on to tell her sad story. She got involved in sex in her courting days. She got pregnant. Out of duty, they got married. It was a tragic mistake. She tried for 10 long years to make it work, but could not. She was finally divorced and left with two small children.

What she was saying was this. Had she only known beforehand the facts she learned that morning and had acted on them, it would have saved her many years of living in hell. She felt she should shout to all those around her: "Listen to this. Don't go through what I had to go through."

Frankly, I'm glad she spoke out to the whole group. It may well have made more of an impression coming from a peer who had gambled and lost.

Perhaps the answers to the next two questions will help speak to the need of those in similar plights. They have made mistakes and paid the price, but the scars of guilt and loss of life fulfillment may still be there.

196 I guess I have gone too far in sex. I know that I should not have done what I'm doing. But why do I feel this awful guilt and how do I get rid of it?

Your guilt is well founded. We've seen that all main religions and almost all parents oppose premarital sex. But so does society. About 90 percent of adults in the U.S. think it is usually or always wrong for 14-16 year olds to have intercourse.[1]

So maybe you should *not* get rid of your guilt. If you know you've done something wrong, maybe you *should* feel guilt.

Guilt is not always a bad thing. It is one mark of being human. We human beings can set standards of action and thought for ourselves, and then try to live up to them. No other species can do that.

Guilt is what we feel when we fail to live up to what we expect of ourselves. That is a good thing. We call it our conscience. It is a dear friend. Treat it with respect and keep it alive and well.

Why? Because you can kill your conscience. If time and time again you keep ignoring what your conscience tells you is right, it stops giving you its warnings. It gives up on you. It hardens. If that happens, watch out! You may be in deep, deep trouble. You then will have no higher guide to shape your actions. In extreme cases, such as the hardened criminal, the right seems wrong and the wrong seems right. If you steal and cheat long enough, it no longer seems wrong to cheat and steal. And if you fail to heed your "still small voice," if time after time you go farther in sex than you think you should, then the voice grows ever more weak. In time it may be hushed for keeps. You may be more comfortable then, but be less human. Guilt tells us when we have committed what the Jewish and Christian religions call "sin." And sin has not gone out of style, much as we might think—or even hope—that it has.

To sin means "to miss the mark" that God has set for us. Our personal mark is that goal of behavior we set for ourselves. When we fall short of that goal, we get a swift kick in the conscience. It says: "Hey, you. Shape up. You goofed. You missed the mark again."

So be real sure your wish to get rid of the guilt is wise. Be sure you are not just trying to clobber your conscience so it will no longer pester you. It may be trying to tell you something you ought to know—and heed.

197 I've done some things in sex for which I am now very ashamed and sorry. Do I have to go on living with that guilt?

No, not if you are now sorry for what you did and really want to be free of your load of guilt.

Both Christians and Jews believe that God will fully forgive us if we really repent. But not unless we promise to try our best not to go on sinning. It won't do to say. "Hurry up and forgive me, Lord. I can hardly wait to dash out and do it again." That won't work.

But if we are truly sorry and want to change, there is no act so awful that God will not forgive us.

If I understand the words of Jesus correctly, there is only one sin that God will not forgive. That sin is the wholly calloused conscience. If we have come to believe that the right is wrong, and that the wrong is right, the Lord will not forgive that. God *will* not because God *can*not.

Put another way, if we don't think we've done wrong, we won't repent. And if we won't repent, God can't forgive us. I believe that is what Jesus meant by the unforgivable sin. God is not about to beat us over the head and drag us, kicking and screaming, into forgiveness. We have to want it and ask for it.

If we come to the point where we call the good evil, and call the evil good, then God can't forgive us for that.

But once we *are* sorry, once we *want* to be free of guilt, then we can depend on God to fully forgive us. We can start over. That is part of the "good news." No person can ever sink so low or be so laden with sin and guilt that God won't forgive him or her.

There is one big problem. Even though your worst sins may be forgiven, *the scars of those sins may well remain.* God and your family and friends may all forgive you for having been an alcoholic. But your damaged liver may not. You may get full forgiveness for foolish sex mistakes. But the sad, sordid scars of sexually transmitted disease, an unwanted pregnancy, or a botched abortion may go with you, or even send you, to your grave.

But take heart. There is still hope, even with scars from the past. We can, despite our despair, claim victory in our lives. We can if we will.

We can pray for and get the inner power to face the future, come what may. Once we have God's forgiveness, then we can forgive ourselves. We can resolve to live life to the fullest in spite of our scars or problems. With God's help we can overcome. The past is past. The future lies before us. There is no need to brood over or mourn what cannot now be changed.

And there's more. We can be a witness to others. Like the woman who stood up in my workshop, we can help others profit from our mistakes. We can forewarn a younger sister or brother or a friend, and guide them from making the same mistakes.

As a college student I once worked in a national forest as a mountain lookout. The trails were steep and rough. Rocks and sticks on the path were potential causes of an accident for me or some future hiker. We learned to flick those rocks and clutter off the trail with our boots as we went along.

In that same way, we can all help clear the trail of life for those who come after us. It's a good feeling.

It is not possible in one book to answer all the questions young people and their elders ask about sex, dating, and love. These queries run into the thousands. What I have tried to do is to pick out those that are most often asked and those that seem most important.

You will no doubt have questions that have not been covered here. If so, seek out the answers. If you are a young person and have parents you can talk to, turn to them. If not, find some other trusted adult. It may be a pastor, rabbi, or youth leader. It may be a counselor or teacher in your school or college. Lots of people out there are willing and able to help. So find someone you can trust and check it out.

Another source of good facts about sex is your library. Public or school librarians may have some suggestions. Religious bookstores and some church libraries can also be explored.

In any case, I hope this book has helped you. May you have a life filled with joy and satisfaction and peace.

You deserve it.

PREFACE

1. Jan E. Stets, "Cohabiting and Marital Aggression: The Role of Social Isolation," *Journal of Marriage and the Family* 53 (August 1991): 669.

PART 1

1. June M. Reinish with Ruth Beasley, *The Kinsey Institute New Report on Sex* (New York: St. Martin's Press, 1990) 92.
2. Reinish, *Kinsey New Report,* 1990: 76.

PART 2

1. Reinish, *Kinsey New Report,* 1990: 85.
2. Shere Hite, *The Hite Report* (New York: Dell, 1976) 612-613.
3. Reinish, *Kinsey New Report,* 1990: 211.

PART 3

1. Update, *Family Planning Perspectives,* (New York: The Alan Guttmacher Institute) 23 (September/October 1991): 197.
2. Reported in a Marriage and Family textbook used by this author.
3. Brent C. Miller and Tim B. Heaton, "Age at First Sexual Intercourse and the Timing of Marriage and Childbirth," *Journal of Marriage and the Family* 53 (August 1991): 719.

PART 5

1. Ray E. Short, *Sex, Love, or Infatuation: How Can I Really Know? Revised and Expanded Edition* (Minneapolis: Augsburg, 1990).

PART 6

1. Reinish, *Kinsey New Report,* 1990: 88.
2. Hite, *Report,* 1976: 591.
3. Association Films, 333 Addaide St. West, Toronto, Ontario, CANADA M5V 1R6.

PART 7

1. Ray E. Short, *Sex, Love, or Infatuation,* 1990: 189-190.

PART 8

1. Brent C. Miller, "Families, Science, and Values: Alternative Views of Parenting Effects and Adolescent Pregnancy," *Journal of Marriage and the Family* 55 (February 1993): 14, from data in Moore, Snyder, and Daly, *Facts at a Glance* (Washington D.C. 1992): Child Trends.
2. Brent C. Miller and Kristen A. Moore, "Adolescent Sexual Behavior, Pregnancy and Parenting: Research through the 1980s," *Journal of Marriage and the Family* 53 (November 1990): 1026.
3. Brent C. Miller, "Adolescent Sexual Behavior," 1990: 1026.
4. Miller, "Adolescent," 1990: 1026.
5. Kathryn Kost and Jacqueline Darroch Forrest, "American Women's Sexual Behavior and Exposure to Risk of Sexually Transmitted Diseases, *Family Planning Perspectives* 24 (November 1992): 247.
6. Associated Press Release, "Rising Spread of Teen AIDS Alarms House Committee," in Chicago *Daily Herald,* April 12, 1992.
7. AP, Chicago *Daily Herald,* April 12, 1992.
8. Thomas Ewin Smith, in review of Thomas P. Gullotta and others, (Eds) *Adolescent Sexuality* (Newbury Park, CA: Sage Publications) 1993.
9. Update, "A Swing in Attitudes on Swinging," *Family Planning Perspectives* 24 (November/December 1992): 242.
10. Ira Robinson and others, "Twenty Years of the Sexual Revolution, 1965-1985: An Update," *Journal of Marriage and the Family* 53 (February 1991): 217.
11. Brent C. Miller. "Adolescent Sexual Behavior," 1990: 1026.
12. For further information, contact: (1) Campaign for U.N. Reform, 713 D St. SE, Washington, D.C. 20003, Ph. 202-546-3956

(a political action group); and (2) World Federalist Assn., 418 7th St. SE, Washington, D.C. 20003, Ph. 1-800-HATE WAR. Both seek a stronger U.N. that can bring terrorists, hijackers and drug smugglers to justice.

13. Randal D. Day, "The Transition to First Intercourse Among Racially and Culturally Diverse Youth," *Journal of Marriage and the Family* 54 (November 1992): 749-762.

14. Brent C. Miller, "Families, Science, and Values," 1993: 15-16.

15. Freya L. Sonenstein and others, "Levels of Sexual Activity Among Adolescent Males in the United States," *Family Planning Perspectives* 23 (July/August 1991): 162-163.

PART 9

1. Ray E. Short, *Sex, Love, or Infatuation,* 1990: 121.

2. Brent C. Miller, "Families, Science, and Values," 1993: 13.

3. Tom W. Smith, "Adult Sexual Behavior in 1989: Number of Partners, Frequency of Intercourse and Risk of AIDS," *Family Planning Perspectives* 23 (May/June 1991): 102-107, reporting a National Opinion Research Center survey.

4. Reinish, *Kinsey New Report,* 1990: 129-130.

5. Reinish, *Kinsey New Report,* 1990: 465.

6. John D. Williams and Arthur P. Jacoby, "The Effects of Premarital Heterosexual and Homosexual Experience on Dating and Marriage Desirability," *Journal of Marriage and the Family* 51 (May 1989): 489-495.

7. Digests, *Family Planning Perspectives,* (September/October 1991): 234-235.

8. Shere Hite, *Hite Report* (Dell, 1976): 613.

9. Reinish, *Kinsey New Report,* 1990.

10. Ray E. Short, *Sex, Love, or Infatuation,* 1990: 111-113.

11. Dawn M. Upchurch and James McCarthy, "Adolescent Childbearing and High School Completion in the 1980s: Have Things Changed?" *Family Planning Perspectives* 21 (September/October 1989): 199-202.

12. Reinish, *Kinsey New Report,* 1990: 18-19.

PART 10

1. Brent C. Miller, "Families, Science, and Values," 1993: 12.
2. Brent C. Miller, "Adolescent Sexual Behavior," 1990: 1025.
3. *Alan Guttmacher Institute,* "Facts in Brief," (New York: 1989).
4. *Guttmacher,* "Facts," 1989.
5. Holly S. Ruch-Ross and others, "Comparing Outcomes in a Statewide Program for Adolescent Mothers with Outcomes in a National Sample," *Family Planning Perspectives* 24 (March/April 1992): 66-71.
6. Holly S. Ruch-Ross, "Comparing Outcomes," 1992: 66-71.
7. Beth C. Weitzman, "Pregnancy and Childbirth: Risk Factors for Homelessness?" *Family Planning Perspectives* 21 (July/August 1989): 175.
8. Debra Kalmuss, "Short-Term Consequences of Parenting Versus Adoption Among Young Unmarried Women," *Journal of Marriage and the Family* 54 (February 1992): 80-90.

PART 11

1. Brent C. Miller, "Adolescent Sexual Behavior," 1990: 1031.
2. William D. Mosher and James W. McNulty, "Contraceptive Use at First Premarital Intercourse: United States, 1965-1988," *Family Planning Perspectives* 23 (May/June 1991): 108-116.
3. Brent C. Miller, "Adolescent Sexual Behavior," 1990: 1031.
4. Brent C. Miller, "Adolescent Sexual Behavior," 1990: 1031.
5. Martha Williams-Deane and Linda Potter, "Current Oral Contraceptive Use Instructions: An Analysis of Patient Package Inserts," *Family Planning Perspectives* 24 (May/June 1992): 111.
6. Spotlight, "Delaying Pelvic Exams to Encourage Contraceptive Use," *Family Planning Perspectives* 24 (May/June 1992): 136.
7. Brent C. Miller, "Adolescent Sexual Behavior," 1990: 1025-1044.
8. Brent C. Miller, "Adolescent Sexual Behavior," 1990: 1031.
9. William D. Mosher, "Contraceptive Use," 1991: 108.
10. Update, *Family Planning Perspectives,* 24 (September/October 1992): 195.
11. "Can You Rely on Condoms?" *Consumer Reports* (March 1989): 135-141; Also see *Mariposa Foundation.*

12. James Trussell and others, "Condom Slippage and Breakage Rates," *Family Planning Perspectives* 24 (January/February 1992): 22.

13. Update, "Beware of Smog," *Family Planning Perspectives* 21 (January/February 1989): 55.

14. Reinish, *Kinsey New Report,* 1990: 363.

15. Koray Tanfer and others, "Condom Use Among U.S. Men, 1991," *Family Planning Perspectives* 25 (March/April 1993): 61-66.

16. Update, "Female Condom: Mixed Reaction," *Family Planning Perspectives* 24 (November/December 1992): 243.

17. Reinish, *Kinsey New Report,* 1990: 357.

18. Digests, "Oral Contraceptive Use Linked to Chlamydial, Gonococcal Infections," *Family Planning Perspectives* 21 (July/August 1980): 190.

19. Carol S. Weisman and others, "Consistency of Condom Use for Disease Prevention Among Adolescent Users of Oral Contraceptives," *Family Planning Perspectives* 23 (March/April 1991): 71.

20. Martha Williams-Deane, "Current Use," 1992: 111.

21. Reinish, *Kinsey New Report,* 1990: 372-375.

22. Reinish, *Kinsey New Report,* 1990: 14.

23. Reinish, *Kinsey New Report,* 1990: 371.

24. Reinish, *Kinsey New Report,* 1990: 371.

25. Update, "The Come-Hither Glance," *Family Planning Perspectives* 23 (May/June 1991): 100.

26. Willard Cates, Jr. and Katherine M. Stone, "Family Planning, Sexually Transmitted Diseases and Contraceptive Choice: A Literature Update—Part I," *Family Planning Perspectives* 24 (March/April 1992): 75.

PART 12

1. Digests, "Adolescent Drug Users More Likely to Become Pregnant, Elect Abortion," *Family Planning Perspectives* 24 (November/December 1992): 281-282.

2. Emily Rosenbaum and Denise B. Kandel, "Early Onset of Adolescent Sexual Behavior and Drug Involvement," *Journal of Marriage and the Family* 52 (August 1990): 783. See also Brent C. Miller, Adolescent Sexual Behavior, 1990: 1027-1028.

3. Update, "One in Four Women 18-44 Smoke," *Family Planning Perspectives* 24 (January/February 1992): 3.
4. Update, "Risks for Cervical Neoplasia," *Family Planning Perspectives* 24 (November/December 1992): 242.
5. Update, "Smoking and Ectopic Pregnancy," *Family Planning Perspectives* 24 (May/June 1992): 98.

PART 13

1. Reinish, *Kinsey New Report,* 1990: 70.
2. Reinish, *Kinsey New Report,* 1990: 470-472.
3. Special Report, "An Ounce of Prevention . . . STDs and Women's Health," *Planned Parenthood Perspectives* 23 (July/August 1991): 175. Also *Kinsey New Report,* 1990: 464.
4. Reinish, *Kinsey New Report,* 1990: 475.
5. Reinish, *Kinsey New Report,* 1990: 492.
6. Reinish, *Kinsey New Report,* 1990: 489-490.
7. Program Spotlight, "Widespread Screening Seeks to Lower Chlamydia Prevalence," *Family Planning Perspectives* 24 (May/June 1992): 135-136.
8. Reinish, *Kinsey New Report,* 1990: 493-495.
9. Reinish, *Kinsey New Report,* 1990: 471.
10. Reinish, *Kinsey New Report,* 1990: 471.
11. Reinish, *Kinsey New Report,* 1990: 471.

PART 14

1. Reinish, *Kinsey New Report,* 1990: 501.
2. Update, "The First 100,000 AIDS Cases," *Family Planning Perspectives* 21 (September/October 1989): 197.
3. Update, "The Second 100,000," *Family Planning Perspectives* 24 (March/April 1992): 50.
4. "The Second 100,000," *Family Planning Perspectives,* 1992: 50.
5. June M. Reinish and others, "High-Risk Sexual Behavior Among Heterosexual Undergraduates at a Midwestern University," *Family Planning Perspectives* 24 (May/June 1992): 116.
6. Kathryn Kost and Jacqueline Darroch Forest, "American Women" 1992: 244.
7. "The Second 100,000," *Family Planning Perspectives,* 1992: 50.

8. Update, "HIV Transmitted by Breastfeeding," *Family Planning Perspectives* 23 (November/December 1991): 245.

9. Reinish, *Kinsey New Report,* 1990: 501.

10. Reinish, *Kinsey New Report,* 1990: 466.

11. Update, "Signs of Poor Condom Use," *Family Planning Perspectives* 24 (May/June 1992): 99.

12. William R. Grady and others, "Condom Characteristics: The Perceptions and Preferences of Men in the United States," *Family Planning Perspectives* 25 (March/April 1993): 67.

13. Leighton C. Ku and others, "The Association of AIDS Education and Sex Education with Sexual Behavior and Condom Use Among Teenage Men," *Family Planning Perspectives* 24 (May/June 1992): 101.

14. Freya L. Sonenstein, "Levels of Sexual Activity," 1991: 162.

15. Update, "AIDS Risk Among Runaways," *Family Planning Perspectives* 23 (May/June 1991): 101.

16. Digests, "Sexually Active Adolescents Have Less Knowledge and Less Fear of HIV than Their Abstinent Peers," *Family Planning Perspectives* 24 (May/June 1992): 142.

17. Leighton C. Ku and others, "The Association," 1992: 100-106.

18. Leighton C. Ku and others, "The Association," 1992: 100-106.

19. Update, "Are Teens Getting the HIV Message?" *Family Planning Perspectives* 24 (November/December 1992): 243.

20. Tomah High School, Tomah, Wisconsin.

PART 15

For sources for 1984 "Profile of Unwed Live-ins," see Appendix 2. For sources for update, see Appendix 3.

PART 16

1. Brent C. Miller, "Families, Science, and Values," 1993: 14.

References to "Fornication" in the Bible*

A. In the Old Testament (equivalent to: Playing the harlot; unfaithfulness; idolatry)

1. Genesis 38:24a
2. Genesis 38:24b
3. Leviticus 21:9
4. Deuteronomy 22:21
5. 2 Kings 9:22
6. 2 Chronicles 21:11
7. Isaiah 23:17
8. Ezekiel 16:15a
9. Ezekiel 16:15b
10. Ezekiel 16:26a
11. Ezekiel 16:26b
12. Ezekiel 16:29

B. In the New Testament (refers to every kind of sexual intercourse outside marriage)

13. Matthew 5:32
14. Matthew 15:19
15. Matthew 19:9
16. Mark 7:21
17. John 8:41
18. Acts 15:20
19. Acts 15:29
20. Acts 21:25
21. Romans 1:29
22. 1 Corinthians 5:1a
23. 1 Corinthians 5:1b
24. 1 Corinthians 5:9
25. 1 Corinthians 5:10
26. 1 Corinthians 5:11
27. 1 Corinthians 6:9
28. 1 Corinthians 6:13
29. 1 Corinthians 6:18a
30. 1 Corinthians 6:18b
31. 1 Corinthians 7:2
32. 1 Corinthians 10:8
33. 2 Corinthians 12:21
34. Galatians 5:19
35. Ephesians 5:3
36. Ephesians 5:5
37. Colossians 3:5
38. 1 Thessalonians 4:3
39. 1 Timothy 1:10
40. Hebrews 12:16
41. Hebrews 13:4
42. Jude 1:7

43. Revelation 2:14
44. Revelation 2:20
45. Revelation 2:21
46. Revelation 9:21
47. Revelation 14:8
48. Revelation 17:2a
49. Revelation 17:2b

50. Revelation 17:4
51. Revelation 18:3a
52. Revelation 18:3b
53. Revelation 18:9
54. Revelation 19:2
55. Revelation 21:8
56. Revelation 22:15

NOTE that the word for premarital sex in the Bible (fornication) is used at least 56 different times. Every time it is used it is strongly condemned. Jesus considered it such a serious sin that he listed it right along with murder and adultery (Matt. 15:19; and Mark 7:21) as did St. Paul (Rom. 1:29; Gal. 5:19).

---

*Some translations use different words for fornication, such as sexual immorality, debauchery, whoremonger, unchastity, impure.

This research is from: Ray E. Short, *Sex, Dating and Love: 77 Questions Most Often Asked* (Minneapolis: Augsburg Publishing House, 1984), pp. 71-74.

Sources for the research on the use of "fornication" in the Bible

ADAMS, A. D., C. R. Irwin and S. A. Waters, eds. (Alexander) *Cruden's Complete Concordance of the Old and New Testaments.* New York: Holt, Rinehart, and Winston, 1949. (p. 232)

AMERICAN Bible Society. *World's Concordance of the Holy Bible, King James Version.* New York: World, 1969. (p. 169)

BUTTRICK, George Arthur, ed. *The Interpreter's Dictionary of the Bible.* Vol. 2. Nashville: Abingdon, 1962. (p. 321)

ELLISON, John W., ed. *Nelson's Complete Concordance of the Revised Standard Version Bible.* New York: Thomas Nelson, 1957. (p. 663)

HARTDEGEN, Stephen J., ed. *Nelson's Complete Concordance of the New American Bible*. Nashville: Thomas Nelson, 1977. (p. 397)

MILLER, Madeline S. and J. Lane. *The New Harper's Bible Dictionary*. New York: Harper & Row, 1973. (p. 206)

Morrison, Clinton. *An Analytical Concordance to the Revised Standard Version of the New Testament*. Philadelphia: Westminster, 1979. (p. 211)

SPEER, Jack Atkeson, ed. *The Living Bible Concordance, Complete*. Poolesville, Md.: Poolesville Presbyterian Church, 1973. (p. 333)

STRONG, James. *The Exhaustive Concordance of the Bible*. Nashville: Abingdon, 1980. (p. 364)

THOMAS, Robert L., ed. *New American Standard Exhaustive Concordance of the Bible*. Nashville: Holman, 1981. (p. 435)

YOUNG, Robert. *Analytical Concordance to the Bible. 22nd American Edition*. New York: Funk and Wagnalls, 1955. (p. 368)

Sources for the 1984 Profile of Unwed U.S. Live-ins

ARAFAT, I. and C. Yorburg. "On Living Together without Marriage." *Journal of Sex Research* 9 (May 1973): 97-106.

CLATWORTHY, Nancy Moore. "Living Together." In *Old Family/New Family: Interpersonal Relationships,* edited by Nona Glazer-Malbin. New York: VanNostrand, 1975. pp. 67-89.

GLICK, Paul C. and Graham B. Spanier. "Married and Unmarried Cohabitation in the United States." *Journal of Marriage and the Family* 42 (February 1980): 19-30.

LYNESS, Judith, Milton Lipetz, and Keith Davis. "Living Together: An Alternative to Marriage." *Journal of Marriage and the Family* 34 (May 1972): 305-312.

MACKLIN, Eleanor D. "Nonmarital Heterosexual Cohabitation." *Marriage and Family Review* 1 (March/April 1978): 2-10. See also her "Students Who Live Together: Trial Marriage or Going Very Steady?" *Psychology Today* (November 1974): 53-59 and "Heterosexual Cohabitation among Unmarried College Students." *Family Coordinator* (October 1972): 463-471.

NEWCOMB, Paul R. "Cohabitation in America: An Assessment of Consequences." *Journal of Marriage and the Family* 41 (August 1979): 597-602. "Olday found that cohabitation was not a more effective screening device than traditional courtship patterns. This contradicts the commonly held notion that one of the potential positive outcomes of cohabitation is improved mate selection." (p. 599)

OLDAY, D. "Some Consequences for Heterosexual Cohabitation for Marriage." Unpublished doctoral dissertation, Washington State University, 1977.

WATSON, E. L. Roy. "Premarital Cohabitation vs. Traditional Courtship: Their Effects on Subsequent Marital Adjustment." *Family Relations* 32 (January 1983): 139-147. ". . . a significant difference in mean marital adjustment scores (in the first year of marriage) was found. Contrary to our expectations, however, non-cohabitors had higher scores. . . ." (p. 145)

Sources for Update on Cohabitation in the United States

1. Bumpass, Larry L., James A. Sweet and Andrew Cherlin, "The Role of Cohabitation in Declining Rates of Marriage," *Journal of Marriage and the Family* 53 (November 1991): 913-927.

2. Carpenter, Wayne D. "College Cohabitors and Non-Cohabitors Twelve Years Later," comparing changes from 1972 to 1982, in Ph.D. Unpublished Dissertation at the University of Syracuse, New York, 1982.

3. Dahn, Joan R. and Kathryn A. London, "Premarital Sex and the Risk of Divorce," *Journal of Marriage and the Family* 53 (November 1991): 845-855.

4. DeMaris, Alfred and William MacDonald, "Premarital Cohabitation and Marital Instability: A Test of the Unconventiality Hypothesis," *Journal of Marriage and the Family* 55 (May 1993): 399-407.

5. DeMaris, Alfred and K. Vaninadha Rao, "Premarital Cohabitation and Subsequent Marital Stability in the United States: A Reassessment," *Journal of Marriage and the Family* 54 (February 1992): 178-190.

6. Manning, Wendy D. "Marriage and Cohabitation Following Premarital Conception," *Journal of Marriage and the Family* 55 (November 1993): 839-850.

7. Schoen, Robert and Robin M. Weinick, "Partner Choice in Marriages and Cohabitation," *Journal of Marriage and the Family* 55 (May 1993): 408-414.

8. Stets, Jan E. "Cohabiting and Marital Aggression: The Role of Social Isolation," *Journal of Marriage and the Family* 53 (August 1991): 669-680.
9. Teachman, J.D., J. Thomas and K. Paasch, "Legal Status and the Stability of Coresidential Unions," *Demography* 28 (1991): 571.
10. Thornton, A. "Cohabitation and Marriages in the 1980s," *Demography* 25 (1988): 497.